A Better World for Our Children

A Better World for Our Children

Rebuilding American Family Values

Dr. Benjamin M. Spock

CONTEMPORARY BOOKS
A TRIBUNE NEW MEDIA/EDUCATION COMPANY

Front cover photograph by Mark Wallack

This edition is reprinted by arrangement with National Press Books, Inc.

Published by Contemporary Books, Inc.
Two Prudential Plaza, Chicago, Illinois 60601-6790
Manufactured in the United States of America
International Standard Book Number: 0-8092-3187-5
10 9 8 7 6 5 4 3 2

Dedication
To Mary Morgan

Who can always tell me where to find my pencils;

Who kept track of a thousand wandering pages of manuscript and helped to organize them into a book;

Who never forgets an appoiontment or a pill;

Whose expertness as chef makes eating a delight, who has magically improved my health and strength with exercises, meditation and group therapy;

Whose energy and cheerfulness are inexhaustible;

Whose compliments on my speeches and writings are my strongest inspiration;

Whose love fills my life; and

Whom I love dearly.

Acknowledgments

I will always be grateful to Nancy Sturdee of Camden, Maine, for keeping me on track during the long years that I have worked on this book, and Lynda Long, of St. Thomas, Virgin Islands, for her skill in typing, reading my writing and finishing the manuscript.

I want also to thank my agent, Robert Lescher, and four editors: Glen Ruh, Alexia Dorszynski, Sally Squires and Jessica L. Weiss, and Talia Greenberg for the index.

And I would like to thank Joel D. Joseph and Alan Sultan of National Press Books for their efforts in publishing this book.

Contents

Acknowledgments vii

Introduction to the Paperback Edition 7

Preface: What This Book Is—And Isn't—About 15

Chapter One: Where I'm Coming From 19

Learning Values 19

Growing Up 23

Medical School 25

Baby and Child Care 27

My Teaching Career 29

A Social Activist 30

The Permissive Label 32

Serious Politics 33

A Full Life 34

Turning Point 36

Responsibility for Your Own Health 37

My Daily Routine 38

Therapy 40

PART ONE:
What We've Got

Chapter Two: The New Social and Economic Realities . . . 45

Depersonalization of Work . . . 49

Changing Lifestyles . . . 50

Excessive Competitiveness . . . 52

Creating Winners or Losers? . . . 55

Materialism . . . 57

Instant Gratification . . . 59

Chapter Three: Sex, Marriage and Family Life . . . 61

Unstable Marriages . . . 62

The Depersonalization of Sexuality . . . 64

Escaping to Drugs . . . 66

Cigarettes . . . 67

Our Overly Mobile Society . . . 69

The Repetitive Chain of Social Maladjustment . . . 70

Chapter Four: Violence and Brutality . . . 73

Video Mayhem . . . 75

Children and Television Violence . . . 77

Chapter Five: Deteriorating Health . . . 83

Diet and Exercise . . . 84

Controlling Chaos . . . 87

Playing, Not Just Winning . . . 88

PART TWO:
Back to Basic Values

Chapter Six: What Happened to Our Standards and Beliefs? 93

Are We What We Wear? 94

Backing Away From What Was Considered Beautiful 95

Who Sets Our Values? 97

Bringing Values Back 98

Chapter Seven: The Roots of Idealism. 103

A Child's First Influence 104

Independence Versus Dependence. 105

Overestimating the Parents 107

Turning to Impersonal Interests 109

The Emotional Tasks of Adolescence 113

The Conflicts of Sexuality. 114

Chapter Eight: Instilling Values 119

Where Do Spiritual Values Belong? 121

Transmitting and Reinforcing Values 123

Can Idealistic Values Survive? 124

PART THREE:
Creating a Better World

Chapter Nine: Toward a Better World 129

Strengthening the Family 129

Strengthening Our Schools 131
Strengthening Jobs and Communities 132
Citizen Participation 133
Chapter Ten: Better Families 135
Spirituality in the Family 136
Religion as a Binder of Families 137
Making High Tech Work for Families 140
Substitutes for Parental Care 142
More and Better Day Care 142
Stepparenting 144
Aids to Family Solidarity 147
Chapter Eleven: Raising Children to Be Kind 151
Maintaining Helpfulness 152
Too Many Gifts 155
Reciprocity 156
Violence and Loveless Sex 157
Sibling Rivalry 158
Discipline Through Love 161
Chapter Twelve: Better Schools 163
Learning by Doing 164
Getting Past Grades 166
Part-time Teachers 168

Qualification at Every Level 170
Relieving the Pressure 171
Making Schools Meaningful 173
Money and Maturity 174
Making Your Voice Heard 176
Getting Values Back in the Schools 177
Chapter Thirteen: Better Workplaces. 181
Apprenticeships 181
Programs that Work 183
Day Care at the Workplace 185
Chapter Fourteen: Better Citizens 189
Citizen Activism. 196
Political Choices 199
Involving Children. 200
Chapter Fifteen: Can We Make a Better World for Our Children? 203
Notes 207
Index 209

Introduction to the Paperback Edition

During the past two years I have spoken before many groups about how we can make the world better for our children. The response has been heartening. Millions of Americans agree that our children are in jeopardy and that something must be done to improve our neighborhoods, day care and schools. I am also encouraged that hundreds of newspapers and television programs have covered my views. I think that most Americans realize that something dreadful is happening and that we must change the way we raise children in this country. The first step in dealing with a problem is to recognize that we have a problem. America has taken this first step. However, we have a long way to go to make a better world. This book is my view on how to accomplish that. I hope that each one of you will get involved by emphasizing helpfulness, kindliness and lovingness in your children; by setting a positive example; by playing an active role in your communities; by asking television networks and advertisers to provide inspiring programs; in a word, by becoming much more politically active citizens.

During the discussion periods after my talks, there is usually someone in the audience who remembers my despair at how things were when this book was originally published in 1994 and who asks whether I am now as pessimistic as I used to be or whether I see more cause for optimism.

I grew up an optimist. (Some say that optimism depends on whether as an infant one felt well fed and well loved.) I've always been deeply moved by children's potential for honesty, generosity, spirituality and lovingness. That was basically what inspired me to go into a child-care profession. (Of course, as we all know, children can also be stingy, deceitful, materialistic and mean—in spells or permanently. But that is usually in response to how the world is treating them—at the moment or regularly.)

Well, I believe we and our children could make this world a wonderful place to live in if we really tried. I am intensely impatient, however, because instead our world and our country are still blundering on. Wars are still raging, not, as some people say, because the itch to fight comes to the surface in ordinary people at intervals, but mainly because aspiring leaders see the opportunity to manipulate the citizens by harping on old hurts and stirring up new suspicions.

On the other hand, I now see a little hope on the horizon. Centuries-old conflicts in the Middle East and Northern Ireland seem to be headed toward solutions. Even in Bosnia a peace treaty has been signed. But peace is fragile. We must be ever vigilant.

The recession keeps lingering on, with ups and downs, ups mainly for the wealthy, downs for the poor and those on modest incomes. The poor get blamed for the debts of government programs—welfare, Medicare and Medicaid, abortions for poor women, housing and social security for old people.

Our economic situation has been called a "winner take all" system. For the first time in my lifetime home ownership is down in America. For the average working American the standard of living has not improved during the past 20 years, and for many it has declined. Yet salaries in the executive suites have increased dramatically. Even when a major corporation loses money its leadership often takes embarrassingly large incomes. "Downsizing" is hailed as a progressive step in the 1990s. This is playing havoc with families. Working parents now have to worry constantly about losing their jobs. It seems that many of us are working harder for less pay and spending less and less time with our children.

The same "winner take all" philosophy has taken charge of athletics. Top professional athletes are making millions of dollars annually while our schools are closing athletic departments. Athletic shoe companies are paying fortunes for endorsements while inner-city families are spending scarce dollars on basketball shoes rather than medical insurance.

The government immunization program for children is being cut. So are funds for day care for poor children, aid to schools and loans for capable but financially limited university students.

Since their congressional election victory of 1994 the Republicans have been determined to cut these programs, with the rallying cry of balancing the budget and cutting income and capital gains taxes. If they were honestly concerned with justice for all citizens, they would have increased taxes for industry and the wealthy. And they would have drastically reduced the defense budget now that we have no major "enemy." Instead they offer the defense department expensive weapons that it did not even ask for.

When I see news photographs of congressional leaders smiling happily at each success while depriving the poor, the old, the sick, children, pregnant women seeking abortions and the homeless, it horrifies and angers me. Some Democrats, seeing Republican successes, ape their stands. Very few offer vigorous, humane leadership. Yet the Republican "sweep" of 1994 was carried out by only 19 percent of eligible voters. Where were the other 81 percent? Where are they now? What's the use of democracy if it's not used? Part of the answer is that many of the poor are cynical because so few politicians' promises have been carried out. And that's because industry and the wealthy have the money with which to win elections for their candidates. Other deprived citizens simply don't recognize their strength in numbers, at least until they are desperate or they find courageous leaders.

On the family level the tragic problems persist. Divorce is still sought as if it were a solution to marital strains. Actually, second marriages end in divorce as often as first marriages do. Divorce disturbs the children for at least two years and is loaded with problems for the mothers and, to a lesser extent, fathers. It is only a solution to the degree that each spouse comes to discover, usually through counseling, what his or her own contribution to the failure was. (It is always easy, inviting and obscuring to try to put the full blame on the other spouse.) Even higher rates ensue when divorce becomes more common and more accepted. And children assume that they too will turn to divorce if there are dissatisfactions in their future marriages. The answer, it seems to me, is for each couple contemplating divorce to seek counseling. If one partner declines to go, the other can still learn a lot, perhaps enough to make a fresh start, for the sake of both partners and the children.

I still believe that we should bring up our children with much greater emphasis on being generous and serving others, much less on getting ahead and acquiring more possessions.

This doesn't mean scolding them, nagging them or humiliating them, as so many parents assume. Children want more than anything else to be like their parents when their parents are in a good and affectionate mood. Parents need to keep this in mind and set a good example. In addition, they need to show real appreciation of the admirable things their children do. This has a powerful effect. They can show authentic pleasure when their two-year-old wants to set the table; when she carries out more complicated chores through the preschool and elementary school years; when, in adolescence, she thinks of volunteering in a hospital or tutoring a younger child.

When a child in a grumpy mood neglects her chores, it is important for the parents not to angrily act as if their previous approval was conditioned on her obeying them. Instead, they can sit down in a serious but affectionate manner and explain how helpful her contribution has been and how disappointed the hospitalized patients (for example) will be if she doesn't show up.

I now believe that children should be firmly but politely reminded, when they are fighting or calling names, how painful this can be to the victims, and asked to think what would be a better way to settle the dispute. It's a mistake, I think, for the parent to interrogate the battlers to try to find out who started it and put the blame on that one. Each thinks that the other was at fault and will argue forever.

I think that parents should not stir up competitiveness but tone it down, not compare siblings but show appreciation for the good qualities in each.

In regard to games and athletics, parents, teachers and coaches should show appreciation of cooperation and improvement more than of winning.

Schools and universities should forget grades—they teach the wrong lessons. I've seen it done successfully in two medical schools.

Parents should keep track of their children's television watching and absolutely forbid violent or crudely sexual shows. I was pleased that Senator Bob Dole and others launched a campaign against these television programs and their advertisers. This is not censorship any more than laws against actual violence are. It is protection for our children. Our children are now exposed to thousands of violent episodes on television and at the movies every year. This not only makes children more prone to violence themselves; it hardens them, desensitizes them and makes them think that brutality is a natural part of life. This is not so in Japan, in many European countries or even in nearby Canada.

I believe that parents should decline to buy toy guns

for their children, saying simply that there is too much killing in the world to make a game of it. America is now in the grip of a destructive movement to arm itself. Concealed-weapons permits are commonplace. At the same time our prison population is growing enormously. We have the highest percentage of people in prison of any democracy in the world. And we are building more prisons, as if that could be the answer.

America is in crisis and our families are at risk. This book is a call to action for Americans to say, Hold on! What are we doing to our children? We must work together to make our day care, our schools and our television better, our neighborhoods safe and peaceful places to live and our workplaces more accommodating to the family. I'm sure all of these steps can be carried out—but only if we first recognize the extent of the problems and that the solutions are within our power as parents and citizens.

Benjamin Spock
January 1996

Preface

What This Book Is—And Isn't—About

This book isn't a manual on the daily care of individual children, like *Baby and Child Care.* It is about the deterioration of our society and what caring men and women can do to leave a better world for *all* our children.

The issues I raise in this book have concerned me for many years—as a physician, as a parent and grandparent, as an educator and as a political activist.

When I look at our society and think of the millions of children exposed every day to its harmful effects, I am near despair. My despair comes not only from the progressive loss of values in this century, but from the fact that our present society is simply not working. Societies and the people who live in them fall apart if they lose their fundamental beliefs, and the signs of this loss are everywhere:

- The increasing instability of marriage, reflected in divorce, single-parent families and stepparenting;

- The over-competitiveness that dominates many fields, and that causes overly ambitious men and women to neglect their children, spouses, friends and communities;
- Inexcusable inequities and discrimination against women and minorities that still persist;
- An exclusive desire for materialism without any offsetting spiritual or ethical values;
- The deadening impact of mindless kinds of jobs in offices as well as in factories, stifling workers' creativity and sense of accomplishment;
- The increasing number of single parents—mostly mothers—who have to work outside the home for economic reasons but who would rather take care of their preschool children;
- A lack of high-quality day care to provide adequately for preschool children's physical and emotional needs;
- The failure of schools to reach children at all levels of ability and to prepare them for productive, satisfying lives;
- The progressive coarsening of the society's attitude toward sexuality, which is caused mainly by television, films and popular music; and
- The steady increase in brutal behavior, including murders within the family and spousal and child abuse, not just by adults but also by teenagers and young children.

These trends can be reversed; but first we have to analyze them and work on correcting them. That is what this book *is* about.

I am troubled by problems many people seem to assume are impossible to change: the widening gap between rich and poor, growing unemployment and homelessness, ineffective elementary and high school education and our dismally high infant mortality rates.

Most important, I believe that the keys to a better world for our children and ourselves are:

- ☐ to reassert the importance of spiritual values—honesty, love of family, respect for others and a sense of idealism that inspires us to strive for greatness in our chosen endeavors;
- ☐ for parents to rear their children with love and understanding, teaching them by their own example the ideals of helpfulness, kindliness and service to others;
- ☐ to make employers more responsive to the needs of families, including flexible work hours and day care at the workplace;
- ☐ for schools and universities to replace outmoded curriculums and teaching methods, and emphasize "learning by doing" and apprenticeships; and
- ☐ for citizens to participate more in community improvement programs and become actively involved in seeing to it that our elected officials are responsive to the needs of families.

But before we can think of ways to rebuild society, we need to recognize just how and why our society has lost its way. After determining what we have done wrong, we can correct our course and start making a better world for our children.

Benjamin Spock
Camden, Maine
July, 1994

Chapter One

Where I'm Coming From

Born in 1903, I have lived in every decade of the twentieth century. I was the oldest of six children, raised in a family where our mother was the dominant influence—for me anyway. I remember little of my first five years, except the delicious taste of baked potato with milk on it. By three I had taken on a wistful, mildly anxious look that I ascribe to my sensitivity to the frequent warnings and scoldings of my moralistic, controlling mother. She loved her babies extravagantly but was alarmed when in their second year each of her children showed signs of wishes and wills of their own. Two of her four daughters became determinedly independent, but her two sons were to a large degree submissive to her will.

Learning Values

We were born in a three-bedroom house with a sleeping porch that accommodated three of us. Fresh air was considered a cornerstone of health then, at least in New England.

My mother cared for us. Our father was a railroad lawyer who worked downtown in the "Yellow Building." He made the short trip twice a day on the trolley. His mother and married sister's family lived six blocks away. My mother's married sister and her family lived five blocks away in the other direction. My mother and her sister led or pushed their children up the Canner Street hill every afternoon to have tea with their mother.

Families like ours took long vacations for the children's sake. We spent three months every summer in a small fishing village in Maine because the cold air was considered healthy. Our father visited us every other weekend. Since the general store in Maine carried no fresh foods, except peas, string beans and corn during their brief Maine seasons, my father made quite a ceremony of displaying fresh vegetables and fruits he brought from New Haven. In return my mother would have secured a boiled lobster, a crock of baked beans and a steamer of brown bread, of which the children could have just a taste because these foods were not recommended in Dr. Holt's *Care and Feeding of Children.*

There was no radio or television. Movies crept in during my later childhood, but there was no chance that I would be allowed to attend. We read constantly—Mark Twain, Dickens, Thackeray. As the oldest, I was taken to hear Rachmaninoff play and watch Pavlova dance. All of us saw *Peter Pan.*

Religion did not play much of a role in our lives. We children went to Sunday school as a matter of course with other children in the New Haven, Connecticut, neighborhood, but our parents did not belong to a church or attend regularly until I was in college at Yale. Mother then required that my sisters attend Yale's compulsory Sunday chapel service and sit in the balcony, to inspire the students with a picture of wholesome young womanhood.

In raising me, my sisters and brothers, my mother emphasized morality. She taught us that sex was wrong and harmful in all aspects, except when intended to conceive babies. She dearly loved babies. There were problems in her own family that amply explain her anxiety. She confided in us as adults that one of her sisters had had a baby out of wedlock, and her own father—a dashing, ne'er-do-well fellow—had frequently deserted his large family and was presumably promiscuous.

These family secrets certainly were enough to explain mother's mistrust of sex. She taught us that sinful thoughts were as harmful as deeds, and to touch ourselves "down there" was not just sinful but might cause birth defects in our children. After four years of medical school and four residencies, I thought I had long outgrown such teachings, but I recall when our first child was born I returned from the hospital's nursery to my wife's room to exclaim happily, "Mike has ten fingers and ten toes!"

As a child, I believed that my mother had the magical ability to read minds because she could immediately detect wrongdoing by any child. Only later did I realize that she had implanted such a strong sense of guilt in me that when I occasionally did something slightly naughty, my hang-dog expression was a dead giveaway. Then she had no hesitancy in asking, accusingly, "Benny, what have you been doing?" It never occurred to me to try to deceive her. To do so would have only doubled my sin and my punishment. I received practically no physical punishment as a child, although I can recall being spanked on the hand with a hairbrush a couple of times. Mother efficiently achieved discipline with her brood by a combination of warnings, shaming and occasional deprivation. Guilt was the worst.

A good example of mother's stern moral teaching occurred during World War I when I was 14 years old. Civilians were supposed to conserve wool for the war effort, and my parents decided that I should wear one of my father's cast-off suits—which naturally was anything but the style young men were wearing. I nearly cried. "I can't wear that," I said. "Everybody at school will laugh at me!" And they did.

My mother was firm. "You ought to be ashamed of yourself, worrying about what other people will think of you. All you have to know is that you are doing the right thing." At 14, of course, I didn't believe her. But 51 years later, when I found myself indicted, convicted and sentenced to two years in federal prison for vigorous opposition to the war in Vietnam, I was comforted to recall my mother's words. I could say to myself, "It doesn't matter what President Johnson thinks as long as I know I'm right about the illegality, the unconstitutionally of the war in Vietnam." I knew that my mother would have agreed.

But, I also remember how she devoted her existence to her children. From the day I was born until my youngest sister went away to Vassar, she gave up bridge, at which she had been a whiz. She had a great sense of humor and delighted her children and her friends with stories about things she found amusing or ridiculous. She was a terrific mimic. She inspired her children with idealism and a drive to serve—five out of six of us became teachers or psychologists.

When asked about my father, a railroad lawyer, I always find myself answering, "He was grave but just." By *just* I meant that I never detected the slightest unfairness or arbitrariness in his judgments. By *grave* I meant that he always seemed serious. I was in awe of him. My sisters remembered him differently. When they describe him, they glow, saying, "He was a darling!" and "Don't you remember? He called us by pet names!" Then I would recall that he usually called me Benno, that he once took me to New York to hear an opera, and to Maine to look over a summer cottage he was considering renting. Yet I still think of him as grave, remembering the shame I felt when I let the coal furnace go out when he had left it in my care, or when the family car was stolen after I had borrowed it during a college football victory celebration and left the key in the ignition. But Father never reproached me. He only looked *grave*. I hated to feel that I had disappointed him.

Growing Up

During childhood I was timid—afraid of rough boys, dogs and possible kidnappers. When I was five, a friend had me convinced that a dinosaur lived at the foot of his cellar stairs. As an adolescent, I thought of myself as a reluctant mother's boy, an image I was determined to outgrow. In college I wanted to become a regular guy—a "big man on campus" if possible—and be elected to a secret senior society, as my father had been.

I attended Andover Academy for two years, and when I won a coveted *A* by placing third in the high jump in the Exeter meet and was elected to a fraternity, I felt I was on my way. Acceptance to Yale—also located in New Haven—was a source of pride, but my hopes were dashed when my mother decided that I should live at home rather than on campus. I needed "to recover my ideals," after I boasted in a letter to her that a girl had called me attractive. My mother loved me dearly, but she felt that compliments could be deeply corrupting.

Yale had just gotten a new crew coach who taught a stroke that depended on height. Through a combination of lucky circumstances—my height of 6 feet 4 inches, as well as a taunting invitation of the varsity crew captain—I worked my way up from the 13th freshman crew to the junior varsity in my sophomore year and to the varsity in my junior year. Our crew won the 1924 Olympic trials in Philadelphia, and at the Paris games that summer we earned gold medals. Meanwhile I had been tapped for a senior society. It couldn't have been a more exciting or significant series of triumphs for me. I felt like one of the boys at last.

At this time in my life I was still shy with girls, and the ones that interested me were equally shy. Then I met Jane Cheney, the first woman who both appealed to me and took me seriously. We traded views on politics—I was a Republican and she an idealistic admirer of Norman Thomas, the socialist—and on psychology, about which I knew next to nothing. I remember Jane confidently informing me that babies' personalities were partly formed by two or three years of age, and I said that couldn't possibly be true.

Medical School

As an undergraduate, I had worked for four summers at a small home for crippled children, earning $50 a month. There I watched an orthopedic surgeon perform an operation that made a ten-year-old polio victim's leg usable, and I was inspired with the idea of becoming a children's doctor. I'm sure that a stronger, deeper motivation came from being the first child in my family and identifying with my mother in her great love of babies.

But medical school was a let-down after the glories of college and the fascination of English literature, in which I majored. I found studying such information as the muscular attachments to the collar bone acutely depressing. After two years at Yale Medical School, I wanted to marry Jane and transfer to Columbia University in New York. When I said as much to my father, he looked genuinely surprised and asked, "On what?" I had to say, "Well, on you, father." This time it was my mother who came to my rescue. She didn't believe in long engagements and she persuaded father to pay the $600 tuition, which I thought excessive after Yale's $250. Jane would continue to work and receive her allowance. She was 20, fresh from two years at Bryn Mawr College, and I was 24.

We lived in a Greenwich Village walk-up, enjoying the big city as only financially strapped newlyweds can. As a married man, I found I was highly motivated to study and led my class in the third and fourth years at Columbia University's College of Physicians and Surgeons. Jane worked at Presbyterian Hospital taking family histories for a research study until our son Michael was born in 1933. Eleven years later, John was born.

After Columbia, I took a two-year internship in medicine at Presbyterian Hospital and a one-year residency in pediatrics at New York Nursery and Child's Hospital. That year I came to the most independent decision in my life—that to be able to give wise advice to the mothers of my patients, I should have some sort of psychological training. There was no such training for pediatricians then, so I took a residency in psychiatry at New York Hospital.

My psychiatric patients suffered from such problems as schizophrenia and manic depressive psychosis, which had no visible connection with the questions a mother would ask a pediatrician. But I did learn one valuable thing during that year: the staff members who could make sense out of our patients' behavior had been psychoanalytically trained. So I decided that as I started my pediatric practice the following year I would also begin psychoanalytic training. This involved personal analysis, two evening seminars a week for five years, and the analysis of a patient under the close supervision of a training analyst.

I learned a great deal from the analysis of my patient, but he learned very little from me. If I had been able to help make an unhappy person happy and productive, I might well have shifted my career from pediatrics to psychoanalysis. When I discovered how difficult that can be—and learned, on the other hand, that mothers were delighted to find a pediatrician interested in such common problems as thumb sucking and resistance to weaning or toilet training—I decided to stay in pediatrics. That was a momentous decision, as it turned out, because it led to my writing *Baby and Child Care* and all that followed as a result.

Baby and Child Care

Because of my psychological training and my particular interest in the everyday psychological problems, two publishers sought me out. In 1938 I had been in practice for five years—and had one child of my own—when Doubleday asked me to write a parents' guide on the physical and psychological sides of child-rearing. I said quite sincerely that I didn't know enough. I was still trying to reconcile Freudian concepts with what mothers were telling me about their babies, about breast-feeding, weaning and toilet training. There was no doubt in my mind that Freud and the babies were both right, but it took years for me to find the way to reconcile them.

For example, I remember hearing in a seminar that a lifelong tendency to depression could sometimes be blamed on weaning a baby from the breast too early or too suddenly. Breast-feeding was not at all popular with mothers in the 1930s, yet the few mothers who tried hard to breast-feed told me that their infants who were offered both breast and bottle in the first few weeks invariably preferred the bottle to the breast. It took me years to care for enough breast-fed babies to learn that babies who have been exclusively fed on the breast for several months feel very strongly about staying on the breast, even though they will take juice from a bottle.

In 1943 an editor of Pocket Books asked me to write a book and said, half jokingly, "It doesn't have to be a very good book because at 25 cents a copy we can sell ten thousand every year." Far from feeling insulted, my perfectionist side was relieved, and the prospect of ten thousand copies a year appealed to the do-gooder in me. After ten years of practice, I was confident that I knew enough to give helpful advice about the most common problems of child-rearing that bother parents.

On the other hand, I was afraid that other physicians would think I had gone too far—that much of my advice, such as the benefits of pacifiers, which were considered unhygienic and repulsive by most college-educated people then, was newfangled and unsound. So when *Baby and Child Care* began selling three-quarters of a million copies a year without any advertising—and was welcomed by a great majority of physicians—Pocket Books and I were both delighted. Still, the royalty rate was so low that I only received a modest amount per year for the first few years.

My Teaching Career

The publication of *Baby and Child Care* immediately changed my life from being a practitioner to being a teacher. By this time, the need was beginning to be recognized for a psychological component in training pediatric residents and medical students, and I was one of the very few who could fill the bill. I was invited to teach at Wayne University in Detroit, at Children's Hospital of the East Bay in Oakland, and at the University of Minnesota's Mayo Clinic. I chose the Mayo Clinic, partly because I wouldn't have to raise the money for the program myself. As in two later teaching jobs, I served primarily on the staff of the department of psychiatry, at the invitation of the department heads, so that I would not be hamstrung or buried out of sight if the pediatric staff proved unsympathetic.

This fear was not unrealistic. Top-level professors of pediatrics in many medical schools had a fundamental, unconscious uneasiness about dealing with feelings. Their temperamental make-up and their natural interest in impersonal aspects of disease—disturbances in body chemistry, unusual immune reactions, invading bacteria and viruses—make them skeptical about emotional disorders and about doctors who focus on them.

After four years at the Mayo Clinic, the director of the child development and preventive pediatric program in which I spent half my time died. I found that our program would have to get along on less money. At the same time, I was approached by the newly appointed head of psychiatry at the University of Pittsburgh about starting a program in child psychiatry and child development. I was glad to accept but, after four years, found that I was not an administrator and resigned.

In 1955, I accepted an invitation to join the departments of psychiatry and pediatrics at Western Reserve University in Cleveland. I was drawn by a radical "new curriculum" that assigned each first year medical student to follow a pregnant woman through her delivery and then follow the baby's development. I also organized a joint study by pediatricians and psychoanalysts of some still-controversial aspects of child development—the same persistent difficulties with breast feeding, resistance to weaning and toilet training, the meaning of "security blankets" and stuffed animals that I had written about in *Baby and Child Care*. I taught happily at Western Reserve for twelve years until I reached retirement age in 1967.

A Social Activist

In 1962, while I was teaching at Western Reserve, I was invited for the third time to join the board of the National Committee for a Sane Nuclear Policy, which was then pressing for a nuclear test ban treaty between the U.S. and the Soviet Union. I had declined to join SANE twice before, on the grounds that I was no expert on radiation and fallout and that I was a reassurer, not an alarmer of parents. By the third invitation I had become much more concerned about the dangers to children of continued nuclear testing and of nuclear war itself. I was convinced that speaking out on these issues was a pediatrician's obligation. So I joined the national board of SANE, became an increasingly active spokesman for the disarmament movement, and was elected a co-chairman.

At first I was flustered when reporters thrust microphones under my nose and demanded to know what I was doing on a picket line or speaking at a disarmament demonstration, as if I'd been caught in some disgraceful act. I was afraid they'd ask detailed questions for which I didn't have answers. But I gradually learned that I knew more than most reporters about disarmament or the harm of radiation. I also learned that if the person being interviewed doesn't know the answer to the question, he or she can shift the subject. Although I started my political career very dependent on the staff of SANE, I gradually became more independent and sometimes gave answers to the media that the staff disagreed with.

Right after retiring from Western Reserve in 1967 I was approached by Lyndon Johnson's campaign committee to do some radio and television endorsement for his re-election. While Republican candidate Barry Goldwater advocated massive bombing of Vietnam, Johnson promised not to send American men to fight in the war, so I often spoke for him in radio and television interviews. But within two months of his election Johnson broke his promise, starting the bombing of North Vietnam and the build-up of American fighting troops in Southeast Asia. Their numbers eventually reached a half a million, of whom more than 50,000 died.

I was outraged. I considered the war totally unjustified, illegal, unconstitutional, and contrary to our promises to the United Nations. My country was committing what I and many others considered war crimes. I wrote indignant letters to the President and redoubled my antiwar activities. In the succeeding eight years of the war I was invited by students to speak at more than 800 colleges and universities; many of them were turning against the war and wanted to hear the views of an older person.

In 1968, along with four others including the Chaplain of Yale University, I was indicted for "conspiracy to counsel, aid and abet resistance to the military draft." We were convicted and sentenced to two years in prison and a $5,000 fine. The conviction was reversed on appeal, and I did not go to prison, although I did spend single nights in jail on a dozen occasions for committing non-violent civil disobedience.

The Permissive Label

A couple of weeks after my indictment, I was accused by Reverend Norman Vincent Peale, a well-known New York clergyman and author who supported the Vietnam War, of corrupting an entire generation. In a sermon widely reported in the press, Reverend Peale blamed *me* for all the lack of patriotism, lack of responsibility, and lack of discipline of the young people who opposed the war. All these failings, he said, were due to my having told their parents to give them "instant gratification" as babies. I was showered with blame in dozens of editorials and columns from primarily conservative newspapers all over the country heartily agreeing with Peale's assertions.

Many parents have since stopped me on the street or in airports to thank me for helping them to raise fine children, and they've often added, "I don't see any instant gratification in *Baby and Child Care*." I answer that they're right—I've always advised parents to give their children firm, clear leadership and to ask for cooperation and politeness in return. On the other hand I've also received letters from conservative mothers saying, in effect, "Thank God I've never used your horrible book. That's why my children take baths, wear clean clothes and get good grades in school."

Since I received the first accusation twenty-two years after *Baby and Child Care* was originally published—and since those who write about how harmful my book is invariably assure me they've never used it—I think it's clear that the hostility is to my politics rather than my pediatric advice. And though I've been denying the accusation for twenty-five years, one of the first questions I get from many reporters and interviewers is, "Doctor Spock, are you still permissive?" You can't catch up with a false accusation.

Serious Politics

In 1972, when the Democratic candidate Hubert Humphrey challenged President Nixon, I became the candidate of the national People's Party, a coalition of ten small independent state political parties dedicated to the principles of cooperation, feminism, and world peace. I had no desire to be president, but I was certainly disillusioned with the Democratic and Republican parties and agreed that it was important to train independent political leaders. Our annual conventions of independent-minded idealists in their twenties and thirties were intensely educational for me. In the end, we won 80,000 votes in the ten states in which we were able to get on the ballot.

I was delighted with the idealism, the independent judgment, the interest in civil rights, disarmament, and world peace in so many of the young people I met during the Vietnam War years. I thought it would be the beginning of a fundamental shift towards a more cooperative society. So in the years after American troops were withdrawn from Vietnam, I was shocked to find that a new generation of college students was uninterested in the great causes that had enflamed their older brothers and sisters. They said their first interest was in getting good grades and then good jobs.

The speaking invitations from undergraduate committees that had occupied me for eight years declined precipitously. Instead, I received invitations from hospital staffs, child welfare organizations, and organizers of lecture series for parents. I continued to write a regular magazine column about common child rearing problems and the startling changes in our society—the increase in divorce, in teen pregnancy and suicide, in drug abuse and violence.

A Full Life

I have had four careers, each related in some way to children's health. First I was a practicing pediatrician, which culminated in my writing *Baby and Child Care*. That book brought me into education, with successive positions at three medical schools and a readership in the millions. My concerns about the arms race and its inherent danger to children—and about their need for more high-quality day care, better schools and health care—made me a political activist. I have also been a father to two sons, a grandfather to five and stepfather to one daughter.

I'm still only half-retired and, with the assistance of collaborators in clinical practice, I continue to revise *Baby and Child Care* every eight to ten years. That's a long, hard job because of the many changes in medical practice and in our society. The feminist revolt of the 1970s leveled severe criticism at me for some of the things I'd written, as well as for the way I wrote them. It took me several years to understand the accusations and then to revise the book, including revising all the pronouns.

In retrospect I can see that I was not a sensitive husband, and Jane, like many doctors' wives, accused me of always considering my patient's needs more than those of my family. After 48 years of marriage, when both our sons were independent, Jane and I separated and eventually divorced.

In 1976 I married Mary Morgan, an Arkansan with an energetic and determined personality. She had heard me speak in Little Rock and was impressed not by the talk but how I handled the questions and by my oversized hands. As an organizer for psychological training programs for health personnel, she signed me up for a weekend workshop where we fell seriously in love. We first lived on boats in the British Virgin Islands and Maine, but later built a house in Arkansas so that Ginger, Mary's daughter, could live close to her other family.

Mary has since taken on all the executive aspects of my speaking and writing career. Since 1988 we've been dividing our time between the Virgin Islands and Camden, Maine. We also spend at least a month on the road in fall and spring, speaking and consulting with publishers, agents, relatives and friends.

When I'm on the road speaking, there is always someone in the audience who asks, "Dr. Spock, how did you get to be 90 and still feel so good?"

I've been practicing transcendental meditation twice daily since my late seventies.

I swim every day, and I try to take short walks after meals. I go to bed at 9 p.m. and get up at 5 or 6 a.m. I do 30 minutes of Yoga stretches each morning. Mary gives me daily massage for my weakened legs.

I've been eating a macrobiotic diet for two years. It includes practically no fat, no meat, no sugar and no dairy products. I lost fifty pounds in the first few months and I was eating as much food as I wanted.

Turning Point

Until a few years ago, my health had gradually deteriorated, beginning with a heart arrythmia at age 65. In 1987 my heart stopped altogether, long enough to drop me face first on the marble floor of the Copley

Plaza Hotel in Boston. So they sewed a pacemaker under my skin, with an electric wire into my heart to keep it beating adequately. Three years ago I had a brief stroke-like episode that reduced my talk to gibberish for 15 minutes, and I was put on a blood thinner to prevent a more serious stroke. My legs were gradually getting weaker and less coordinated; the neurologist said it would be progressive. For a year I had repeated attacks of severe bronchitis that required antibiotics; that scared my internist.

In 1991, I was introduced to a Belgian-trained physician who had become a macrobiotic counselor. He put Mary and me on a macrobiotic diet. He and other counselors recommended daily meditation, swimming, walking, stretching exercises, massage, and group discussion of everyday problems.

I've had no bronchitis in the three years since. My leg strength is slowly improving. I feel more alive and alert. After dropping fifty pounds, I lost all my subcutaneous fat, so I get cold easily; I understand now why old people want a shawl. After three years of consistent exercise, massage and diet, I now have regained 80 percent of my original coordination and strength, and I can walk and swim.

My cholesterol level has gone from over 200 to 123; Mary's was 285 and is now 124. We found that our annual pharmacy bill went from $5,000 to $780.

Responsibility for Your Own Health

Once you decide to take your healing into your own hands, any sense of powerlessness and hopelessness ebbs away. Depressive notions are replaced by a positive sense of "I'm in charge of my own healing process—and I can make a change!"

Our government could do much more than it has done in the past to subsidize health care wisely, but it can only do so much. We citizens are the primary caretakers of our own health. The alternative medicine movement in this country is leading the way by advocating such preventative health measures as good diet, exercise and abstinence from tobacco and alcohol.

I think the macrobiotic life style—it means "great life"—and preventative medicine can be the least expensive, most productive, and most powerful alternatives to our health care plans. But you may have to become more patient. All my symptoms were improved within six weeks, but each individual case is different. The secret is being disciplined enough to be consistent. This isn't a diet you go on for a month, lose ten pounds, then stop and gain 20 back. It's a whole way of thinking differently about your healing process and your life style. It takes on a spiritual quality that most diets or disciplines do not have—the spiritual awakening that comes from the combination of practices.

My Daily Routine

My wife, Mary, and I start our daily routine very early. We wake without an alarm clock, usually between five and six in the morning and begin two or three hours of transcendental meditation, yoga and massage. We first do a warm sesame oil massage, starting with my head and feet, then concentrate on my legs.

Before our transcendental meditation we rest a few minutes, then do 30 minutes of yoga stretching exercises. I have had problems with loss of strength and coordination in my legs, so we do several different positions that stretch the legs and improve circulation. I do leg lifts, and Mary tugs on my legs as if she is pulling them out of their sockets. I do neck and shoulder exercises to improve my stiff neck, which I blame on 90 years of leaning over a writing desk.

We also do arm exercises; I raise my arms up, out and wide open, stretching my chest muscles to increase circulation and to fill the lungs.

After this morning routine, we have a macrobiotic breakfast. We always begin with a miso soup followed by a whole-grain dish—brown rice, whole oats, buckwheat, millet, quinoa, wheat berries, barley or a four-to-one combination of brown rice and the others.

I eat leafy greens three times a day—collards, broccoli, kale, watercress, parsley, bok choy, carrot tops or sprouts—always removed from the heat after two or three minutes so they stay bright green. These greens have been the basic reason for my lung improvement. I have not had bronchitis since I began the diet.

We also have bancha twig tea, a real tea but the twigs do not have caffeine as do the leaves. We sometimes vary the meal to include fried mochi served as a pancake with a touch of raspberries.

Our exercise each day is a 30 minute swim. I wear a wet suit because I lose heat fast. I also use a snorkel and mask because my neck doesn't swivel. I still swim an old fashioned frog stroke, having never really learned a good breast stroke. We also walk for ten to 15 minutes after our meals.

By 9:00 p.m. we are ready to go to bed. By going to bed early, I get more rest and am more alert in the morning. Before the diet and exercise program I would fall asleep and nod off during dinner or at work at my desk. Now I'm more awake and more lively and more clear in my thinking.

Therapy

With this lifestyle change we also do a weekly group therapy session, which we organized for several reasons. When my wife and I were in analysis, we found group therapy a very effective tool for self-awareness. We also found that the group process gave us protection and permission to say and feel things we didn't say outside the group—our level of intimacy has grown deeper between ourselves and with the other group members. In these sessions I always learn something new about myself and Mary that I never knew before.

In general, I look forward to the group and welcome the chance to work on myself. Others in the group point out things about me that I would never admit myself.

I have seen enormous changes in every decade of this century. Some of these changes have been for the good.

But, in retrospect, even more have been harmful, and I am very concerned about the world we are leaving to our children.

PART ONE:
What We've Got

Chapter Two

The New Social and Economic Realities

As the twentieth century comes to a close, this country is still one of the most prosperous and advanced in the world. At the same time, however, our divorce rate has climbed to a dismaying height and the quantity and quality of day care is tragically inadequate. We are the most violent society in the world. We have allowed materialism to eclipse idealism, and overcompetitiveness to harm families and family values. Millions of our people are in fear for the long-term security of their families, and a growing percentage is on the edge of poverty and despair.

For Americans in the top income bracket, the future looks good—for them and for their children. Incomes have gone up dramatically in the past dozen years while in real terms taxes went down. Their standard of living—unlike that of the population as a whole—is still the highest in the world. They have good health care. They can afford the best colleges and universities for their children. Recreation is available in golf clubs, health clubs, children's camps and a multitude of vacation facilities.

For people in the middle-income range, real incomes have stayed about the same or gone down. Inflation has boosted the cost of goods and services, usually more than the increase in wages. During the last decade real wages (wages adjusted for inflation) declined in the United States, the only major nation in the world to suffer such a decline in the standard of living.[1]

Average Americans are awash in material possessions and conveniences that were once looked on as luxuries, but they struggle to keep up with payments and repairs. Just as indoor plumbing and electricity were the symbols of progress a few generations ago, people now take cars, television sets and major household appliances for granted.

In many middle-income households there are now two breadwinners, yet middle America maintains enormous levels of personal debt and low levels of savings. As the nation has shifted from an industrial to a post-industrial economy many people employed at skilled labor have lost their well-paid factory jobs and have had to take lower paying jobs in service industries.

The promise of secure employment and guaranteed retirement—the goal of the American economy following the Great Depression and World War II—has faded. People fortunate enough to have protected jobs, especially in state and federal government agencies (which are not as safe as they used to be), look forward to guaranteed health benefits and pensions. Those in more vulnerable jobs, particularly in manufacturing and other traditional industries, have genuine concerns for the health and well being of their families. Those on low incomes have become distinctly poorer in the same period, and their children's health has deteriorated.

For the first time in the twentieth century, statistics show increases in such diseases as malnutrition and lead poisoning. Vaccination against communicable diseases has actually declined. The market for unskilled labor is gradually disappearing. Many families dependent on public programs for food and health care have been hurt by cuts in school lunch and food stamp programs. The urban poor, always vulnerable to economic and political change, have been victimized in multiple ways. Two to three million Americans have been hit so hard by underemployment and deep cuts in funds for low-cost housing and welfare that they wander the streets, homeless by day, sleeping in parks and over street gratings to ward off freezing at night. It is calculated that this country's homeless population includes 200,000 children, whose personalities will be adversely affected for life. Can you imagine how children feel when they have no home to go to?

The economic picture for the nation as a whole has become shaky. By the early 1990s, budget deficits were in the neighborhood of two to three hundred billion dollars a year,[2] thanks mainly to excessive Cold War armament and unjustified tax reductions.

As the balance of party politics shifted from a Republican to a Democratic presidency in 1992, the national debt remained at historically high levels. The anticipated "peace dividend" envisioned with the collapse of the Soviet empire never materialized. Instead, a shocking number of our large banks and savings and loan associations have had to be rescued by our Treasury and ultimately, the taxpayers, because of unsound or unscrupulous lending practices.

Our balance of foreign trade has never before been so unfavorable, largely because of complacent or greedy industrial leadership here—most notably in the automobile industry. Once the leader in communications and information technology, we are now facing intense competition in this field which is expected to define the world's economy in the next several decades if not the long-term future. In a nation with unparalleled medical facilities, millions find health care out of reach. We are the only developed country with such a failure. Despite our vast national wealth, scientific know-how and technological superiority, disputes have continued about whether to make adequate health care accessible to all citizens, because of the objections of the many vested interests involved. Although we have long since considered basic public education a right of all citizens, we have not granted Americans the comparable right to basic health care.

We are not alone with our problems, of course. In a majority of the developed nations of the world, economies are struggling, too, especially as they affect the working classes. The former socialist countries, which at least provided their citizens a common level of existence, are having a difficult time finding their way in a capitalistic, market-driven world economy. As usual, aggressive self-interest tends to win out, while the working poor can barely maintain minimum levels of shelter, food, education and health services.

Although the Cold War is over, brutal localized conflicts are raging in Europe, Africa and Asia—in ethnic and tribal hostilities, civil wars and international disputes. Some of them receive coverage on prime-time television news, but most go unnoticed. In underdeveloped and poverty stricken countries of the Third World, disease and starvation are still rampant. Yet the knowledge to prevent and cure the diseases is available, and the food could be raised in developed countries including the United States.

Depersonalization of Work

When people live by farming, hunting or fishing, build their own houses, weave cloth, and make their own garments, pots and utensils, they take great satisfaction from the quality of the product they've created. If they make it to sell to someone else, they have the added pleasure of the customer's satisfaction. The fundamental satisfaction that such jobs give in non-industrial societies is usually absent in the industrialized world.

Industrialization has brought a primary concern with efficiency and profit, and thus the assembly line—not just in factories but in large offices. Workers repeat meaningless, monotonous steps a hundred, a thousand times a day. They never see the finished product, so there is nothing to be proud of. They never deal with a client, a customer or a supplier. It is increasingly common in America and in Europe, to hear people's complaints about boring, nerve-wracking, spiritually ungratifying work. The only gratification is the money earned. This is an example of narrowing the satisfactions of our way of life towards purely materialistic rewards.

Changing Lifestyles

The revolutions in communication and transportation that define this century have provided mixed blessings. We take for granted the ability to travel to the next town in a matter of minutes or to another continent in a few hours. We can choose to live many miles from our jobs, in order to escape smoky factories and crowded cities. Cities themselves, once magnets for commerce and culture, are fast becoming undesirable places to live because of high costs, rapidly deteriorating infrastructure and increasing crime. Cars are affordable, enough so that walking has become a leisure activity, not the basic means of human locomotion.

New communities are built without sidewalks, but with acres of paved roads and parking lots. People choose to travel long distances to and from work, even when it means being stuck for hours a day in traffic jams or on crowded buses and trains. We accept the inconvenience, because with it comes the freedom to move far and fast when we want to, for recreation as well as for jobs. But the moving of a family undermines the emotional security of children and adults, as I found in my own family when I moved several times as I was offered more interesting positions at various universities. At the time I failed to consider the impact of these moves on my wife and children.

Electronic communication, despite some of its negative effects, lets us talk with equal ease to people around the corner or halfway around the globe. Businesses, governments and ordinary citizens have access to information and human interaction undreamed of even half a century ago, and the quest for better and faster information exchange keeps going on. Personal computers, modems and fax machines not only make business work faster and more efficiently but allow many people to work in their homes. This gives some parents more flexibility and more time to spend with their children.

Forward-looking employers exploit the new information networks not only for better business but for better relations with their workforce. Job sharing, flexible hours, home offices linked by modem to office computers—all these things can be powerful inducements to improve and strengthen family relationships if people use them with imagination and resourcefulness.

There is, however, a downside: flexible hours and part-time employment let employers sidestep their responsibility for providing adequate employee benefits, including health insurance and adequate day care for children. The trend towards service employment in a post-industrial economy means that competition for well-paying jobs in some sectors is fierce. This keeps salary and benefit levels low, and an aversion to paying taxes has the same effect on government jobs.

Even though there is a superficial national prosperity, many working parents can barely keep pace with the financial demands of raising a family. In spite of technological advances, the fast pace and competitive nature of today's society cuts a certain percentage of the population out of the mainstream. People who cannot cope—for lack of ability, education or opportunity—are forced to live on the margins of society, surviving on welfare. Unemployment, especially among underprivileged and undereducated youth, can lead to frustration, cynicism, dropping-out and crime.

Unfortunately, these negative effects are felt directly or indirectly by children at times in their lives when they most need security, serenity and loving care.

Excessive Competitiveness

Competitiveness—particularly excessive preoccupation with advancement on the job—is one of the most harmful aspects of life in America. The drive to excel at all costs erodes spiritual values in obvious and subtle ways. For parents who work outside the home, constant competitive pressure will upset the balance between job and family relationships. For a parent who stays at home, that pressure can cause chronic resentment about being ignored or neglected. Because parents' tensions are inevitably passed on, full force, to their families, children suffer from diminished attention and affection.

I once had a discussion with two groups of nine- to twelve-year-olds whose mothers and fathers were both professionals or executives. The children were openly bitter about the amount of time their parents spent working at the office or at home at the expense of time with them. I've also been consulted by fathers whose adolescent sons or daughters had gotten into one kind of trouble or another. The men confessed that in their intense preoccupation with businesses or professions they had neglected their children and wives. These fathers realized that they hardly knew their own children.

The competitive spirit also shows up in parents pressuring their children in their schoolwork, demanding that schools give them more homework, emphasizing grades. Working parents—particularly parents fueled by a compulsive need to compete—expect schools and care givers to match their own unrealistic and unreasonable standards, even though they may know little about how effective education works or what their children's teachers are really doing. Preschool and day care teachers report that some parents keep asking why children can't be taught the three Rs at age three or four. More disappointing is that some educators give in to these demands.

One child development institute claims that it can teach reading at age two and assumes that this will be advantageous, but there is no long-range, scientific evidence to support the claim. I suspect that this kind of force-feeding at an early age actually leaves children prejudiced against schooling in general, the very opposite of parents' intentions. I recall a film of a young child being taught to read at two—the child looked like a scared rabbit trying to escape, but he had been cornered by the psychologist.

Some parents are putting too much emphasis on winning at too early an age. Wanting to give their sons and daughters every advantage, they sign them up for lessons or for highly organized leagues for baseball, soccer, basketball, swimming and diving at early ages. These substitutes for natural play often demand expensive equipment and facilities. Sometimes the result is parents and children getting up before dawn to drive them to hockey practice or figure-skating lessons. These highly competitive individual or team sports inevitably put heavy emphasis on winning, not on simply learning a skill and enjoying the game.

City children used to be sent to summer camp to enjoy the outdoors and overcome the pressure of school. Now parents send them to tennis camps, soccer camps, computer camps, math camps—all based on the premise that it's good to give children a competitive edge for success. If they can afford it, parents enroll their children in special social, cultural or athletic activities after school or on weekends. The activities may be beneficial if the children are truly motivated, but oppressive if they are not.

Children like to explore, reject and rediscover different kinds of activities, and it is usually good to let them do so at their own pace. If left alone, they set their own goals and proceed at their own speed. Children naturally want to develop new skills. The most positive kind of motivation—whether it's riding a bike, catching a ball or learning a magic trick—comes from watching and emulating other children or adults. The exercise benefits their health, and the children also learn initiative, leadership, followership and teamwork. But when an overly aggressive coach takes over and constantly exhorts them to win, a lot of the fun and initiative is lost. As an ex-collegiate oarsman, I can testify to the boredom that comes from being scolded for technical faults, season after season, for four years.

Creating Winners or Losers?

Competitiveness in sports, like the satisfaction of playing a musical instrument, builds confidence and self-reliance in young people, if winning is not overemphasized.

Physical activity and learning to play by the rules are important parts of any young person's education. There's a big difference, however, between the joy of games and the adult drive to mold growing children into championship performers. Televised sports and entertainment generally gloss over the grueling aspects of professionalism and focus only on the glamour. It's normal, of course, for children to aspire to succeed like their role models in sports and other fields, as long as they are not pushed to extremes by parents. But it is sad to see a willing young person urged into competition in the unlikely hope of stardom.

There are many examples of children quitting organized teams because they were made to feel inadequate by coaches or parents yelling at them from the sidelines and criticizing them if they made mistakes. In many towns in America, the entire citizenry focuses on the high school basketball and football teams which sometimes give the athletes involved an inflated idea of the importance of their contribution and interferes with their efforts after graduation.

Adults should be teaching children and adolescents that any degree of accomplishment is worthwhile. It is just as important to recognize every able participant as to reward the winner. It is a lot more beneficial for a child to learn good sportsmanship than be ashamed of coming in second best.

The intensity of some contact sports can do irreparable damage to growing bodies. In the worst cases, young athletes turn to pain-killing drugs or anabolic steroids, risking permanent bodily harm for the sake of a varsity letter or a winning season. College teams, particularly those with television contracts and jet-set travel itineraries are professional in all but name. The successful coach earns much more than a professor—in terms of both salary and fame. He or she doles out fortunes to lure promising high school athletes with "athletic scholarships." These fees-for-service corrupt not only the athletes who receive them but anyone who is led to believe that natural talent should be converted into dollars.

My idea of a good sport would be frisbee. You see it being played on college campuses on a Sunday afternoon with women as well as men participating—some flashy, others just novices, but everybody having a good time. But you know as well as I that if it became a major sport in the present atmosphere, the university president would have to budget $100,000 for a coach and other hundreds of thousands to recruit promising high school players.

You may think I'm overemphasizing the harm of competitive sports in high school and college, which in one sense is true. But it is one of the most familiar examples of intensive competitiveness, it contributes to the general atmosphere, and it corrupts millions of youths at least slightly into believing that this is what life is really about. This overemphasis misleads many students into developing physical skills instead of mental skills, making life's highest achievement the dream of joining a professional team. The realization that there is little room at the top comes only after the frustration and disillusionment of being passed over, and sometimes cruelly exploited, for the sake of the school. Too often those students are the ones that might have been encouraged toward less glamorous, more realistic goals.

Materialism

Overlapping our high competitiveness is our materialism. All societies and economies have a degree of materialism, but in many parts of the world (and in America in the past) materialism has been balanced and integrated with spiritual aspirations such as religious beliefs, patriotism or dedication to the extended family. Religion in other times and places has given people an inspiring sense of the meaning of life and guidance in living it.

In the Middle Ages the cathedral towered above the city in every sense. Painting, sculpture and music concerned religious subjects. Even in earlier America the church was the highest, most impressive building and the clergyman was a leader of the community. In Israel most citizens, especially those in the agricultural *kibbutzim* have a strong conviction that they are in the world to build a new nation and to make the desert bloom. These goals for many have a higher priority than individual ambition. It gives a sense of unity with fellow citizens which is supportive and inspiring. In America we rally to our country's defense in war, but take it for granted in peace time.

Novels about European existence, especially in earlier centuries, give us a feeling of the overriding importance of the extended family. Respect was directed from the young to parents and by all to the grandparents. Boys were expected to enter the family business. Decisions about marriage were too crucial to be left to the young.

But in twentieth-century America the young are expected to strike out on their own. Though there continues to be a sentimental attachment to "mom" and some of the other relatives, it often has no functional substance. When I've asked young women expecting their first babies whether they will call their mothers for help, some of them have answered with surprise, "Oh, she'd be too old-fashioned in her ideas to be of any help!" Or, "She'd try to take over the care of the baby."

The focus on competitiveness and materialism in America and the bountifulness of our natural resources have given us, except in economic depressions, an ever rising standard of living, with less and less need for grinding work. Those conditions, along with the lure of advertised products and the weakening of our spiritual beliefs, have gradually shifted our orientation away from the ideas of service, hard work and contentment with limited rewards, towards an ever-expanding desire for money and things.

Instant Gratification

Most Americans have come to expect everything at their disposal instantly. The proliferation of credit cards has fueled these increased expectations. I think this expectation of receiving all good things, with limited effort and no down payment, is one factor in our high and rising divorce rate and in the crime rate among unemployed youth.

In economic depressions and in wartime our rates for suicide and mental illness go down. In wartime, too, people become friendlier with neighbors, more generous and more cooperative. They see what the major purpose in life is, at least for the time being. They are ready to make sacrifices. Citizens are happy to be part of a unified effort for the common good.

In periods of prosperity, when unifying movements are less evident, people turn more greedy and self-centered. I suspect that the main reason why teenage suicides have quadrupled in the past 20 years—surely an indication of serious sickness in society—is a lack of spiritual beliefs.

Young children can count on their parent's wholehearted dedication to them. Adults with jobs and families are stabilized by knowing that they cannot possibly quit either. Adolescents and youth are shedding the remnants of their childhood identities, changing their appearances and all their feelings, but have not yet found their adult identities. Some of them become frightened by such a lack of connectedness, such lack of focus. They may be temporarily obsessed with a religious cult, or a street gang, just the way a drowning man clings to anything that floats. Other causes for despair in adolescents have been the threat of nuclear annihilation and the prevalence of crime, violence, drugs, divorce and dishonesty in high places.

America has entered a new, uncharted economic era. Many families have both parents working and still are worse off than their own parents were a generation ago. Even though we are told that the economy is performing well, major corporations like Sears, IBM and many others are laying off hundreds of thousands of their employees as a part of "downsizing." Employees are working longer hours with no real economic gains. These economic and time stresses have caused intense changes in family life.

Chapter Three

Sex, Marriage and Family Life

The traditional roles of fathers, mothers and children vary a lot in different parts of the world and under various circumstances. I have seen the stability of families and marriages drastically changing during my lifetime. After eight or nine decades I still remember my childhood distinctly.

Parents want their children to remember being cherished as they remember being cherished as children themselves. That's why girls and boys of three and four insistently play house with a younger child or doll. The young baby demands food, love and other needs from the parents. These demands, in combination with the environment, start the pattern of the individual's growth and development that in 20 or 30 years produce a new mother and father to start another family cycle.

If my childhood sounds tame today, it's because it was tame. But in retrospect, I can see that we were made secure by the stability of our life and the closeness of our parents. We didn't know anyone who was divorced and the possibility of divorce in our family never occurred to any of us. We grumbled at the strictness of our mother who was the strictest parent we knew. But there was nothing we could do about it because arguing with her might tighten the restriction or lead to punishment. All the parents we knew in those days were much more sure of themselves and of how they were bring up their children than parents are today.

Of course we cannot return to the "good old days." We cannot get rid of television, video games or divorce. But we can bring back some of those traditional family values and stability.

Unstable Marriages

There are, undoubtedly, a number of causes for the great and increasing number of divorces and unstable marriages. Divorce used to be considered scandalous and this contributed to holding many marriages together despite strains. And conversely, the more common divorce becomes, the more natural and acceptable it seems. Half of all marriages now end in divorce in America.

Another factor, it seems to me, is that we are living in an age when people in general are very self-centered. They focus on what they want and what they think they are entitled to, rather than on what they contribute. You might think that most divorced people would have learned enough to make their second marriages wiser and more stable; but it doesn't work that way unless at least one partner in the earlier marriage has learned what his or her own contribution was.

Once, when speaking to a singles club, I asked how many of the divorced members wished they had tried harder to make their marriages work, more than half raised their hands. This startled me and made me think that probably many divorces are decided on in the heat of a prolonged angry interchange in which the contenders take turns in escalating the criticisms, insults and provocations, and make it harder and harder to back down. So two people who once thought each other supremely attractive—which thus made it easy for each partner to be pleasing—now provoke each other to be skunks.

So the amazing truth is that each of us has the power to make any other person like us or hate us, including a spouse. People seeking a divorce usually think of it as a solution. It rarely is. A divorce is hard on every member of the family. Each of the children shows symptoms of anxiety and resentment for at least two years; some investigators say it's for the rest of life.

The mother, who most often gets custody, may have to seek a paying job outside the home for the first time in her life. This is partly because child support allowances are notoriously inadequate and many fathers fail to make even these payments. The children make more demands on her because their father is absent. She has little opportunity for social life. Finances are strained.

Even the father suffers because, though his income increases, he misses his children. He may be seeing them weekly but they don't turn to him for advice, help or spiritual support. He doesn't feel like a father anymore. On the other hand, there are an increasing number of fathers who are awarded custody of the children.

Men often suffer a similar fate in this situation, with increased financial and emotional strain.

Most divorced people eventually remarry and become stepparents. I discovered myself that being a stepparent is extremely painful for a long time. It's easy enough to advise the stepparent to avoid being a disciplinarian until he or she is accepted as a substitute parent. But when a parent is being endlessly ignored in his or her own home, or spoken to rudely, the parent gets so angry that he or she can't follow such a rule.

Certainly a couple having marital problems should consult a counselor. If one partner won't (perhaps because of an unconscious fear he or she would find out the part he or she is playing in the failure), the other partner should seek the counseling, not to admit that it's all his or her fault, but because one partner's initiative may be able to get the relationship back on track. Unless at least one partner can learn the part he or she is playing in the conflict, a second marriage is likely to founder on the same rocks.

The Depersonalization of Sexuality

Sexuality has also been coarsened and brutalized in our society. I blame in large part the greed of the television community, publishers and movie producers who exploit sexual themes to a degree unnecessary to tell the story, and the television schedulers and advertisers who place these programs for presentation when children and young people are likely to watch.

Parents once worried about their children picking up misinformation about sex "on the street corner." Today, they can have it in the comfort of their own homes, through crass music videos, situation comedies built around bathroom jokes, and the more insidious soap operas and television dramas that celebrate casual sex, marital infidelity and other seamy themes. Knowing where to draw lines about violent and explicit television and movies is complicated for parents, teachers and the general public.

Part of the problem lies in the Supreme Court's difficulty in defining pornography. I blame also—though it was not intentional—the sex education movement itself. It set out, quite wisely, to try to eliminate the ignorance, the fear and the shame that was regularly taught to children. But, the movement usually forgot to present the spiritual and emotional aspects of sexuality. That left little to teach except pure anatomy and physiology.

Preteens and teenagers are naturally curious about their own sexual development, and they feel intense pressure to learn and experiment. If they've heard only the anatomical and physiological aspects of sex, they will see no reason not to experiment. Partly as a result, many teenagers today regard sex not as any part of a spiritual relationship, but as a game of conquest or simply a sensual indulgence. The result has been a sense of casualness and relative promiscuity, higher rates of teenage pregnancy and more sexually transmitted disease.

I believe that whenever a child asks a question related to sex, from age two onwards, parents should explain that sex is part of what makes a man and a woman fall in love, want to get married, help each other, take care of each other and raise fine children together. Then you should discuss the physiology. The depth and details that you discuss with your children varies with their age and sophistication, but love, consideration and kindness should be emphasized.

Escaping to Drugs

Why has drug abuse become not simply a matter of addiction, which is bad enough for every individual, but a widespread epidemic? I can't prove it, but I suspect that one reason is "style." Many societies often go through periods where styles or fads dominate life. This is especially true in America, where our melting pot is not based on one traditional way of life that has persisted through countless generations. The American people come from all parts of the world, immigrants who often thought so little of the old country's traditions that they dared to pull up roots and take a chance on the unknown. Americans have been eager to adopt anything from new clothing styles, dances and games, to the popular ideas of Freud, which were taken up much more in this country than in his native Austria.

Our society is, with the possible exception of Japan, the most tense and competitive nation in the world, so we need some sort of drugging to soothe ourselves. It's indicative that the drug alcohol is more abused in the striving societies of northern Europe than in the happier Mediterranean countries. I believe that if we had a more relaxed, less competitive society, which emphasized the importance of family life and of neighborhood relations, fewer adults and adolescents would need to knock themselves out with alcohol and other drugs.

If I had preadolescent children, I would tell them that they are entering a stage when school is more difficult and there are other internal stresses as their bodies and feelings undergo significant changes. I would tell them that I hope they will get along without alcohol or other drugs, including tobacco, at least until they are 18 or 20, when they are more sure of themselves. Then I wouldn't question or check on them unless there was strong evidence of drug abuse. Drug use is one topic that should be discussed in family meetings and at the dinner table, but lecturing children will often be counterproductive.

Cigarettes

Cigarette smoking has declined in the United States but is on the rise among the young and among women. Cigarette smoking is a filthy and harmful habit. Young children who smoke are harmed directly and nonsmoking children are affected indirectly by their parents' smoking. Parents addicted to cigarette smoking should try to get rid of the habit for the sake of their children.

If you must smoke, do so outside—indoor smoking fumes linger and are breathed in by children and friends. I like the expression that "smoking should be confined to consenting adults in private." With restaurants and other establishments restricting smoking, society appears to be moving in this direction. However, smoking by teenagers in America appears to be on the increase again. I believe that this is caused by peer pressure, the continued glamorization of smoking in print and billboard commercials, on television and in movies. No matter how much parents try, some teens will continue to sneak a smoke.

Most states in the United States prohibit the sale of tobacco to minors. These laws have not been very effective. One of the primary ways that teenagers purchase cigarettes is by vending machines. There is a growing movement to outlaw vending machines for this very reason. I applaud the effort to restrict sales of cigarettes and encourage others to join the movement.

Another positive step we can take to restrict smoking is to drastically increase the tax on cigarettes. Many European countries have substantial taxes on cigarettes. While this has not been effective in keeping consumption there low, a drastic increase in the cigarette tax here, I believe, will help keep cigarettes out of the hands of children. Without high cigarette taxes in Europe, I believe even more smoking would take place there.

A high cigarette tax in the United States could also be used to pay for health care. It is also a reasonable tax to use towards health insurance costs, since smokers have considerably higher health care needs than nonsmokers.

Our Overly Mobile Society

While the quest for financial gain is making the world excessively competitive and materialistic, the competitive business ethic is making our society overly mobile. Families can no longer count on the community roots that they once had. Transient families don't know their neighbors and cannot make lasting friendships. And these frequent moves uproot our children's lives and relationships with their peers, their teachers, and their families.

Corporations expect employees to pack up on short notice and take assignments that keep them away from home for long stretches. Young adults compete for advancement in many corporations that rotate junior executives to different cities every few years. Wage earners feel compelled to trade secure places in the community for job security at any price. This mobile lifestyle is stressful and depressing to most spouses and children, although the results are not always obvious until later in life. It is brutal—emotionally and socially—to uproot families every few years. I eventually recognized this fact in retrospect, because I now realize that I failed to consider the impact on my family of too-numerous relocations.

Over an eight-year period, I changed teaching positions and cities three times. Because each new job was more challenging, I saw only the bright side. I tried to ignore the distress of my wife and the pain of my sons, who didn't want to leave their school and their friends. I'd advise ambitious young men and women to scrutinize all of their employer's expectations—explicit and implicit—to see how much of their own independence of thought and their family's welfare they are being asked to sacrifice. They may decide that firm family roots in a community outweigh the temporary pleasures of a more prestigious job.

The Repetitive Chain of Social Maladjustment

Poverty, social demoralization, irresponsibility, abuse of women and children and other criminal behavior, get passed on from generation to generation with discouraging regularity.

During World War II, I served two years in the Navy as a psychiatrist. Most of my work involved writing the personal histories of sailors who had proved, within a few months of induction, that they were much too irresponsible to be of any use in the armed services.

Their histories were monotonously the same: soon after the child was born, one parent had deserted the family or died, and the remaining parent had to work outside the home. As young children they had been placed by a parent in poor quality day care or in foster care where they received little love or attention from the foster parent. Some of them had been treated roughly.

The effects of the deprivation of love showed up early in school. They had brief attention spans and had no urge to please or cooperate with their teachers. By 14 or 15 years of age they had been held back a couple of grades, were sick of being scolded by teachers, and quit school. Later they tried working, but were inattentive workers, and were fired or quit their jobs.

If one of them committed a minor crime, like stealing a car for a joyride, he was given a choice by the judge—go to jail or enlist in the Navy. When, naturally, he chose the Navy, the judge would add, "Maybe the Navy will make a man of you."

But the armed forces can't make men out of impulsive, irresponsible, self-centered, complaining individuals. After joining, these misfit sailors soon began going "over the hill," with the excuse, "I asked for leave and they wouldn't give it to me." Then, after three or four offenses, when it was obvious that higher fines and longer incarcerations had no effect, they would be admitted to a locked disciplinary ward to await official diagnosis and discharge. "Psychopath" was the usual diagnosis at the time, but today they would be considered sociopaths. Their discharge from the Navy took a number of weeks. After all of this, they were always dissatisfied that they didn't get honorable discharges, as if they had been faithfully serving the Navy and their country.

The pattern of these repeated case histories showed clearly that lack of love in early childhood has devastating effects on character that cannot be repaired by stern discipline.

The same principle applies in any family or community situation and will have the same effect on the children: when parents have no love to give their children, those children grow up to be impulsive, irresponsible and self-centered. If they, in turn, have children, the pattern will be repeated again. The only salvation for such children is for child welfare organizations to detect neglect early in childhood—which is not hard to do—and to provide loving foster care or adoption. But good foster care has to be searched for and paid for while the parents are treated.

For children in families that are only mildly disadvantaged, kindly day care and concerned friendly schools would reduce the likelihood that children will pass on their insecurities to the next generation. Unfortunately such benefits are not widely available. Children growing up in hostile, unloving, deprived families—of which there are many—need to be identified and rescued early. In extreme cases, where parents are truly irresponsible or abusive, the kindest—though the most controversial—solution is to move children to foster homes, at least temporarily, while the parents' anxieties and inadequacies are treated.

Children are affected by a partial lack of love just as much as they are when love is completely absent. In either event that lack of love is often passed on generation to generation. On the other hand love, kindness and caring can also be passed on from generation to generation.

Chapter Four

Violence and Brutality

Our nation is the most violent in the world—much, much more so than the countries of Europe, the Pacific and even neighboring Canada—and it has been getting progressively worse in the twentieth century. The pioneers who settled this country in waves had to be aggressive to pull up roots and to survive in a harsh new land. They not only betrayed, dispossessed and eradicated the Native Americans, but each group of immigrants found ways to insult and abuse the next. The waves of largely European immigrants and generations of their American-born children eventually fashioned a new society. The very multiplicity of the groups now making up our population has contributed to the lack of a common philosophy and to the often hostile rivalry between groups.

African-Americans, starting as slaves, have had to contend with being unable to disguise their race as they've painfully tried to climb the ladder to equality. While many people of color have successful and productive lives, the problem of racial injustice is still with us. Too many young, urban minority males especially feel disenfranchised and cheated by society as a whole. Many minority males have been raised by single mothers who are themselves victims of poverty and other social injustices. The absence of stable parental influences may contribute to a lack of firm family values.

Statistics for murder and other crimes in all sectors of our society are horrifying. Murder, rape and sexual abuse are shockingly high, as is the abuse of children and spouses. These statistics point to the intense stresses and hostilities in our society and the lack of control.

Children may see all manners of horrors in the newspaper and on television news: a plane crashes and the bodies of children as well as adults are strewn on the ground. An insane person opens fire in a crowded restaurant, killing adults and children. Another extremely disturbed person shoots children in their classroom.

You can expect quite a range of responses to the news of such tragedies from different children, depending on age and sensitivity. Children between six and twelve are generally more toughened by knowledge of what goes on in the world. At this age, children are naturally more interested in violent cartoons and television shows than younger children, and therefore somewhat less likely to be upset.

Adolescents are, of course, more familiar with the seamy sides of life and take pride in their sophistication. Even if they are at first inwardly shocked by some distressing event, they quickly try to fit it into their previous picture of the world and act as if they had known about such things all along.

By contrast, children under six tend to be much more sensitive. They know little of what goes on in the world outside their family, so they have little basis for evaluating an unusual experience. They suffer the full impact of a disturbing occurrence because they have no emotional defenses and their feelings are less developed. And much more than older children, they immediately apply to themselves anything fearsome that happens to someone else. I remember vividly how one of my sons at the age of four gazed horrified at a newspaper photograph of a man's head protruding from an old fashioned iron lung. I tried to reassure him by explaining that the man couldn't breathe for himself, and that the machine breathed for him. Suddenly my son grabbed his throat in terror and whispered hoarsely, "I can't breathe!"

Video Mayhem

Though there is no question that the best of computer programs and interactive video products can be superb teaching tools, the reverse is also true: many of today's electronic video games simply encourage a sense of perversity and brutality. Today's video arcades, like pool halls and pinball parlors in the past, are a poor substitute for spontaneous outdoor games that let children burn excess energy and exercise their imaginations. Unfortunately, video games have invaded the home.

Mechanical pinball machines, which were widely abhorred in the 1950s and 1960s, had fairly benign themes such as baseball or bowling. Video games, which were simple and tame when they started in the early 1970s, have taken an ominous direction. Most new video games are dominated by violent themes. Their names give an accurate description: *Mortal Kombat, Total Carnage, The Punisher, Vendetta, Street Fighter II, Hyperfighter, Fighter's Story,* and *Lethal Enforcers.*

In these games children take on the roles of characters like Captain Carnage or Major Mayhem. The predominant goal is to kill or maim an opponent by gouging, smashing, pummeling, shooting, vaporizing, and even forcibly removing major body organs and blood. One game features a muscular man and a well-developed woman in various cops and robbers shoot-outs, urging players to attack the enemy with automatic rifles, shotguns, machine guns, grenades and explosives. Another includes overdeveloped, tattooed males with shotguns killing similarly ugly characters. The female is dressed in skimpy leather underwear and whips the other characters. The winner is the one who kills the most people.

What do children learn from this type of game? It's not that they will go out and commit the same kind of mayhem, but large doses of vicarious violence will condition them to some degree to accept real violence as one of the solutions to life's problems. Tom McDonough, a California Institute of Technology (Cal-Tech) professor who created the best-selling Space Adventure educational computer software, is worried that these games short-circuit the higher functions of the brain, requiring hand-eye coordination with no analytical thought, fueled only by a killer instinct. Parker Page, a psychologist and president of Children's Television Resource and Education Center, said, "It looks like some kids who have a steady diet of playing violent video games may be more at risk of either being more aggressive with other children in the real world, or more tolerant of the aggression around them."[1]

Children and Television Violence

Children vary enormously when confronted by the unfamiliar or the unknown. Some young children, because of their innocence and lack of reality can be disturbed by animated cartoons or simulated television violence as much as by scenes of real life humans. I have seen children at two years of age who became panicky when they fell down or were barked at by a dog. At three they are apt to be scared of the dark.

A few individual children in middle childhood and even in adolescence are easily upset. A movie about a monster or a human fiend may worry them for weeks. If they temporarily lose a parent in a crowd, they may go to pieces. These overly sensitive children are particularly likely to be disturbed by violence on television. Hearing about a kidnapping on television makes them fear the same fate, makes them suspect that any slightly unusual person they see in the street is a kidnapper.

Is there harm in children watching violence, whether or not they are unusually sensitive? I believe we have definite evidence that there are two kinds of harm. The first is that fearful children's fearfulness will be increased and made longer lasting when they are frightened by external events or scenes or stories. The second harm is that average children will be desensitized to violence—will come to feel that it isn't bad, that it's just a normal part of life; this gives them moral permission to beat up their siblings. Those children brought up without much in the way of standards or ideals can be influenced by real or simulated brutality to abuse not only peers but even to commit violent crimes, including murder.

How can you prevent your children from being disturbed by violence on television? If it's a drama or a supposed comedy program with a lot of continuing violence, parents can and should, I believe, matter-of-factly explain to children why they are not allowed to watch. It has been calculated that three quarters of children's viewing of television is in prime time so that is the time to be vigilant about what your children are watching. Parents can check up every few days to make sure the rules are being followed, and let their neighbors know their feelings, to prevent their children from watching with the friend down the street. As children get older, it is a good idea to discuss questionable programming, movies and video games with them during dinner or family meetings. Families can come to a mutual agreement in which the children have a voice about what shows are acceptable.

With television news parents never know when violence will crop up, and it crops up even more in these days of body-bag journalism. It is a shame that news broadcasting has sunk to such a low ebb but commercial interests have come to overrule everything else in television, including responsible news broadcasts. I think that young and middle-aged children should be restricted from watching news programs, unless some program is a special documentary that you feel will be educational and devoid of brutality.

But, you may object, shouldn't children be encouraged to follow the news? I believe that adolescents should be encouraged, but that few under that age are realistically able to learn constructively about the nation and the world from television news or documentaries. If older children seem to be genuinely interested, you can compromise by having children and parents watch the news together.

One of the harms of watching televised news, particularly the real-life on-the-spot police programs now enjoying prime-time exposure, is that children tend to identify with people who are victims in a confrontation, even if there is no explicit brutality shown. When police are shown subduing a suspect or herding people down the street, when strikers or demonstrators are picketing and the police are trying to control them, "law and order" can seem violent—because in many cases in this country, it is.

When children have been disturbed by any kind of horror, real or imagined, the best thing that parents can do is encourage them to talk about what they've seen, what they think caused it and what they are worrying about for themselves. It's better to explore children's own fantasies and dreads first. When parents understand children's fears and concerns, they know better how to go about reassuring them. I say this because kind parents usually have the impulse to reassure quickly, when they have only a vague, general idea of what the fear is. Easy reassurance often misses the target and leaves the child still worrying about his particular fear, that the parent doesn't really understand. Because children's fears may seem quite illogical or irrational, it's hard for adults to imagine what their true worries are.

I recall a psychological study of what worried children hospitalized for a tonsillectomy. A majority assumed that the operation was punishment for wrongdoing—that they had caught too many sore throats because they hadn't worn their gloves or coats or galoshes in bad weather. A child who had been moved to a different room after admission to the hospital was in despair because she assumed her parents wouldn't be able to find her when it was time to go home. A boy thought that in a tonsillectomy the surgeon cut the throat from ear to ear, tipped the head back like the lid on a coffee pot, and reached into the wound to cut out the tonsils. In such cases the parent who offers general reassurances without first finding out the child's specific fears would not be much help.

A recent summary of international figures on handgun murders, a great majority occurring within the family, showed that no European country had more than 40 per year, but the United States had over 11,000. Of course our lack of laws concerning the possession of handguns played a role.

For the wholesale violence that is becoming even greater, I blame television and movies first of all. We know for a fact that the average child has watched 8,000 depictions of murder before finishing elementary school.[2] And each viewing makes the child more callous. As if fictionalized violence is not enough, television is now polluting young minds with so-called police documentaries that depict in grim detail actual crimes and real victims. Any headline-grabbing crime spree is likely to be followed by a no-holds-barred television re-enactment. While these programs give lip service to condemning the grisly events they depict, the cameras continue to focus on the most sordid details.

A well-loved, sensitive child may not be turned into a thug by this diet of aggression and gore, as a neglected or abused child may be, but everyone is being moved toward acceptance of more brutal attitudes. Producers of such shows claim that most viewers, year after year, want to see more violence. Whether or not the producers' claim is true, it does not excuse them for providing so much brutality during children's viewing hours. Only systematic boycotting of the channels and the advertised products gets the attention of the producers of such programming, but rarely are such boycotts sustained by viewers in sufficient numbers to make the media executives take notice. Meanwhile, parents should see to it that their children not watch such programs.

At one point I considered violent play, with or without toy guns, a harmless developmental stage. I changed my mind when an experienced nursery school teacher told me about how her three- and four-year-old pupils were now hitting each other without provocation. When she remonstrated, they said righteously, "But that's what the Three Stooges do." Even though *The Three Stooges* has been around for a long time, more recent television programming is distinctly more violent. In other words, children of three and four are already modeling themselves after adult violent behavior, whether real or simulated.

If you are violent with your children, they are more likely to be violent with their playmates. If you hit them as punishment for a misdeed, a child will learn that violence is appropriate behavior. To reduce violence in society we must eliminate violence in the home and on television.

Chapter Five

Deteriorating Health

There is a new epidemic facing America and the world. It saps the strength of young and old alike, making them fat, passive and lethargic. It clogs the arteries, turns muscle to flab and leaves the eyes glazed over. In adults, it's called the "couch potato syndrome," and far too many children are becoming "couch potato tots."

Before our very eyes, American children are becoming progressively more obese. Since 1960, the frequency of childhood obesity has increased by 50 percent. We now have 12 million overweight children—about one child out of every five. But it is not just an American problem. Twenty-five to 30 percent of Israeli first graders have high cholesterol levels; a quarter of Israeli elementary school children are overweight; and 80 percent can't run half a mile without considerable difficulty.[1] A British study showed that the majority of 7- to 11-year-old children were physically unfit.[2]

Obesity is a serious health risk because it contributes to many physical and psychological problems. It is the leading cause of high blood pressure in children. About 50 percent of obese children have high levels of "bad" cholesterol and low levels of "good" cholesterol. Childhood obesity leads to diabetes, joint disease, menstrual irregularities and other hormonal abnormalities. Cholesterol disturbances carry over into adulthood and lead, years later, to early death from coronary heart disease, stroke and cancer.

The psychological effects of childhood obesity are also devastating. In a society where thin is beautiful, overweight children become the object of jokes and teasing. Gym class can be a daily, painful embarrassment, as can swimming in the neighborhood pool. Overweight children are the last chosen for sports and the first to become social wallflowers.

In many children, these forms of rejection lead to a vicious cycle of overeating, avoidance of exercise, and more eating. It's easy for such children to turn to solitary afternoons filled with television and fat-laden snacks instead of participating with other children in active, calorie-burning play. These experiences in childhood can lead in time to low self-esteem, depression, and an unremitting cycle of poor physical and emotional health.

Diet and Exercise

What causes more and more of our children to be overweight? Disease is rarely the cause. One of the two main causes in children and adults is simply lack of exercise, complicated by large doses of television watching. More lethal still is the tendency toward a greater and greater intake of fat foods—potato chips, french fries, meats, chicken, mayonnaise, butter, cookies, cakes, ice cream, whole milk and other dairy products.

The longer we human beings are on any diet, the more reluctant we are to give it up and change to another. By two years of age children are outgrowing their infantile need for high milk fat, preferably from their mothers. By three years, some of them are beginning to show elevated cholesterol and the laying down of arteriosclerotic plaque in their coronary arteries, a process that, if continued, will result in heart attacks and strokes in middle and older age.

It is usually not necessary for a growing child to lose weight deliberately. The better approach is to slow the pace of weight gain, letting children grow into their ideal weight ranges over time. Besides a wholesome, low-fat diet at home, children need the same thing in schools, and that may require discussion in the PTA and working up the line to teachers, principal and even the superintendent.

When I go to the grocery store and see what is in the shopping carts of people with children, I am in shock. I see parents buying sugar for their children at a rate that would sicken or kill many other animals.

Children are wired with sugar for breakfast with sugar-coated cereal, jam on toast, and sugar in orange juice or hot chocolate. In combination with fats in other prepared foods and caffeine, it constitutes a near-lethal overdose of drugs that sends kids bouncing off the walls. And I consider sugar a drug rather than a food since it has no nutritional benefit except calories. (Some nutritionists dispute the harmful affects of sugar, but none will argue that it is good for you.)

One elementary school teacher told me that a third of her students were on Ritalin—a drug prescribed for hyperactive behavior. While there may be valid uses for drugs like Ritalin, I believe that they are considerably over-prescribed. Adding drugs like Ritalin to the equation is, in my opinion, like stepping on the gas and the brakes at the same time.

One out of five children suffer from obesity and this number is increasing. Our children now have the highest rate of cholesterol ever recorded in history. We are pumping their veins full of junk food, and their hyperactive behavior is a clear result. In the richest country the world has ever known, and with the finest foods of the world available, we do an injustice comparable to overt child abuse when we feed our children the foods that a majority of children are eating regularly today.

Children can in time change their diets if the whole family changes. You can't expect one child to change while the rest of the family continues to eat improperly.

The answer is to minimize the intake of meats, dairy products, fried foods and high-fat snacks. Children should be weaned from milk by about two years, or at least limited to skim milk. Their diet should consist of whole grains and vegetables—including root vegetables and plenty of green leafy vegetables to cover calcium needs–a variety of beans and fruits, preferably cooked. This is the commonest diet among healthy people in the non-industrial world, and children and adults will do well on it in America.

Controlling Chaos

Children can also learn to meditate, which has shown very good results in dealing with hyperactivity. Once the excess caffeine, sugar and fat are eliminated and the diet is balanced with whole grain breads, beans, rice, fresh fruit and vegetables, then the child can be taught to meditate with the parents, eliminating the need for medications like Ritalin. As I discuss later in this book, children respond well to "quiet times," which can include meditation, reading, napping or silent praying.

If the home is chaotic with a television blaring, people shouting, the telephone ringing and people running in and out, the child cannot do anything else but react in kind to the chaos. When the environment and diet change in the home, the tone is set and the sense of calm and relaxation will be reflected in the child. Medications and psychiatric treatment for many hyperactive children simply permits children and their parents to ignore their bad habits.

We owe it to ourselves and our children to offer them something better. A kinder, more relaxed home environment. A meal with loving, nurturing food to go with a loving environment. The most important thing at meal time is to sit calmly and not to rush. You may even want to unplug the telephone, turn off the television, turn down the lights, light some candles, and have a few moments of silence before and after the meal. I know this is different from kids running in, grabbing a piece of pizza and cramming it in their mouths as they rush out the door. But even teenagers will notice when there is a "real" meal on the table.

Playing, Not Just Winning

Natural unorganized play is not as common as it once was among urban and suburban children. Open schoolyards, where children can play in groups before and after school or during the lunch recess, are less and less common. Today students troop off buses straight to class, are herded in and out of lunchrooms in timed shifts, and board buses again when the last bell rings. After school, passive indulgence in television, recorded music and video games takes the place of active, uninhibited play for too many children and adolescents.

School athletic programs are too often based on competitiveness, rather than spontaneous play for its own sake, and focusing instead on the varsity teams. In most towns and cities today you search hard to find sandlot baseball and football games or pick-up basketball. Instead, there are organized youth leagues, burdened by expensive equipment and uniforms, fixed schedules, selective teams rosters, shiny trophies, all dominated by demanding, highly competitive coaches.

I'm not saying that organized athletics and teams sports aren't valuable at the high school and college level. Trained instructors and coaches who aren't obsessed with winning and aren't tyrants can help young people develop not only their physical skills but confidence in their own natural abilities. For teenagers especially, the value of teamwork, cooperation, and camaraderie in a team sport can't be denied. Unfortunately for the students, however, physical education programs concentrate less on the value of play, exercise and camaraderie, than on schedules.

Well-intentioned programs like the Presidents Council for Fitness rely on performance goals and competitive achievement—not the right emphasis in my view, even for self-motivated children. Managed programs can never take the place of spontaneous play for fun and, incidentally, for sharpening individual skills and learning the virtues of teamwork.

PART TWO:
Back to Basic Values

Chapter Six

What Happened to Our Standards and Beliefs?

This century has seen a progressive relaxation of many of our standards of behavior and the souring of many commonly held beliefs. Taken one by one, most are of little importance. Taken together, I believe they show that we have lost our way.

In the nineteenth century, American and European family structure was still formal and hierarchical. Parents and grandparents were accorded deference for their age and experience. The father and mother were recognized as heads of the nuclear family and they presided with dignity. Children were brought up to show respect for their elders.

Today, the family ideal operates under stress, if it operates at all. Single-parent families and broken homes are commonplace. Most of the elderly—unless they are rich—hope merely for tolerance. In many families the father is no longer an impressive figure who presides at meals and in family councils. He tends to be absorbed in his work outside the home. In television comedies the father is often perceived as a buffoon. Mothers are decreasingly seen as dependable, respected nurturers. In some families, the children demand—and get—more attention and respect than the adults. Rudeness and uncooperativeness are often accepted with little protest from their parents.

Meals, which were formerly ritual ceremonies involving the entire family, have become more casual, and in some homes, family meals around a breakfast or dinner table are non-existent. Food comes not in its natural state, but precooked and packaged for convenience and eaten anytime of day. Kids grab something from the refrigerator and eat on the run, anytime they please. Parents may leave for work early and come back late, not preparing and serving their children wholesome, balanced meals, but serving them mainly as chauffeurs.

Are We What We Wear?

I can remember a time when office workers and university students, just like professional men and executives, wore dark suits and stiff white collars. Women were primly clad from neck to ankle. Wardrobes were limited, but everyone dressed in their best to travel.

Today, even some professional men and women wear jeans and casual shirts to the office or traveling. It's commonplace to see people traveling on airlines in shorts and T-shirts with advertisements for athletic teams, shoes, beer or entertainers.

This transformation of clothing styles—a retreat from formality and from wanting to look one's best—has been progressive for a hundred years. Sports and leisure clothing are becoming everyday wear in schools, businesses and even churches. I used to assume that the blue jeans style would pass and that men and women would once again wear clothes of greater variety and formality when not doing chores. But now jeans are actually manufactured with slit knees and made to look old, bleached and rumpled when they are new.

It's interesting to see that the impulse to make a good impression with clothes has not entirely disappeared, even among young people, although it tends to be reserved for ceremonial occasions. Normally grubby high schoolers rent frilly pastel tuxedo outfits and still buy expensive gowns for the annual prom. Women shop with their hair wound up in curlers, so they will look beautiful for parties on Saturday night. I am not concerned with what kind of clothing is appropriate, but with the meaning of such a strong, consistent shift in spirit.

Styles of dress won't stay the same; they never have in the past. But in addition to keeping us warm, the clothes we wear reflect what we think of ourselves and what we think of other people who see us.

Backing Away from What Was Considered Beautiful

Books and other forms of the printed word were once precious enough to be reserved for serious subjects. Now, anything goes in print. In an era of photography, painters have backed away from traditional scenes and still life to concentrate on abstractions, and their human images tend instead toward distortion. Serious music has turned from harmonics to dissonance. Popular music is often shouted or screamed instead of sung, and some of it exhorts its listeners to outright acts of violence or personal degradation. Much contemporary dancing expresses anger and aggression, compared with the mild-mannered, romantic ballroom dancing of yesterday.

Since the turn of the century, there has been a progressive coarsening of language in ordinary conversation, as well as in novels, movies and plays. In the nineteenth century, genteel women sometimes fainted when they heard working men use blasphemous or foul language. Today men and women from every background curse, use foul language, or refer to their own and others' bodily functions. "Why not be honest?" they ask. I believe the answer is that this kind of "honesty" really shows a loss of self-control, self-respect and respect for the dignity of others, as well as a diminished ability to express oneself.

One of the great technological advances in this century has been in communication. Electronic communication—first by telephone and on radio, by mid-century through television, and now by computer networks—has expanded our capacity to share ideas in ways unimagined a century ago.

As a result, we have access to vast and growing stores of knowledge and a keener awareness of the world and the universe. The communication explosion opens doors to the arts and sciences, to personal and professional contacts. Nonetheless, most Americans look on the communications media mainly as a source of entertainment, and take for granted the instant availability of professional sports, comedy, drama and music. Television and films are capable of delivering excellent quality performances, but too often they resort to the lowest kind of vulgarity and brutality.

In all these examples, we can see form and idealism ebbing away from our lives. I believe that this contributes to a general feeling that existence does not have much meaning any more—that instead, it's a catch-as-catch-can affair.

Who Sets Our Values?

In the early days of this country, values were set—primarily and firmly—by the clergy, who were accepted as the leaders of the community, and by parents guided by the clergy. In the more recent past, when I was a boy, standards for children and youths were set mainly by parents but also by friends, older siblings, school teachers and clergy. Few children saw dramatic productions on stage, and the ones they did see tended to be sentimental in spirit. Film was in its infancy; television and videos did not exist.

Studies show that today many, many children and young people get their standards *primarily* from movies and television. These media are so powerful and their messages so convincing that only forceful parents with firm beliefs can counteract the amoral or immoral values they often present. In reality, film producers and writers—and in the case of television, the advertisers who nourish them—are now the primary opinion makers, the value setters for much of our society. But most of them exhibit little sense of responsibility to match the enormous influence they exert. Objections to the glorification of violence, brutality and casual sex in television and movies are met with protestations by civil rights advocates about the chilling effects of censorship, as if that were the only issue.

Anthropological studies from all over the world, to say nothing of the historical record, show that children can be taught any set of values that their parents and their group truly believe in. If children worship material success rather than truth or compassion, it is only because they have absorbed those values from others. To counteract this, it is not enough merely to preach to them. If parents preach morality to their children but behave hypocritically, the children are more likely to become cynics than saints.

Instead, parents must hold to a set of values and maintain their own idealism, so that their children will be inspired by their example. Parents can reinforce their example of idealism by pointing to those figures, both historical and contemporary, who are honest, kind, and idealistic, who remind the rest of society of the existence of those qualities, and who provide leadership in the fight against cynicism.

Bringing Values Back

I suspect that the turn toward fundamentalism in religion that we see today, as well as the rising opposition to abortion and sex education, is not merely the expression of political reaction but also an expression of anxiety about a world going wrong. The people who take strong positions on these issues are the ones who are frightened that everything they were brought up to believe in is being forgotten, if not spurned. They think that the only salvation is to return to the very same morality and standards with which they themselves were raised.

I too believe that our society has misplaced its values and lost its bearings. However, I believe that the solution is not to rush backward, eyes closed, groping for the answers of the past, but instead to look for the causes of our problems and for realistic solutions that might fit those causes.

I believe there are at least three major reasons why so many people in our society have lost their belief in themselves and in the values closest to their hearts.

Christian, Jewish and Moslem religions teach that human beings were created in God's image and for God's purposes. This teaching has traditionally given people a strong sense of purpose and dignity. But the steady expansion of scientific knowledge in the last two centuries—particularly in biology, anthropology and psychology—has undermined the biblical explanation of the world, of humanity's place in it, and of humanity's special relationship to God. The gradual acceptance of humanity's having a less exalted place in the overall scheme of things has, I believe, had a profound and depressing effect. It has deflated our spirits, but so slowly that most of do not recognize how or when it happened.

As valuable as biology, anthropology and psychology are to understanding our human existence, each recognizes only a limited and rather mechanical aspect of humanity. The complexity of the human being is left out, particularly the spiritual and idealistic aspects that differentiate us most from other animals—those aspects once called the soul. This omission has led many people to the cynical conclusion that we should stop worrying about any higher aspirations and settle for enjoyment of our lower, animal nature.

A third reason for our rejection of the standards of the past has been our protest—conscious and unconscious—against the excessive artificiality of the nineteenth century: the overly proper Victorian manners, the denial of our negative emotions, the suppression of sexuality, the emphasis on making a good appearance at any cost. It seems to me that in our degrading language, our tattered clothes, our emphasis on the physical aspects of sexuality we are still, after a hundred years, rebelling against the pomposity and stuffy propriety of our Victorian ancestors.

As powerful as these reasons are, however, I believe we can and should challenge them. Unless a substantial proportion of people hold to positive standards, beliefs and ideals, a society begins to come apart at the seams. We are seeing it happen: materialism unchecked by idealism leads to oppression of the powerless by the greedy; excessive competitiveness hardens hearts even within families; tolerance of violence unleashes all sorts of brutality; acceptance of instability in marriage encourages ever greater instability; the absence of values in children leads to a generation of cynical, self-centered adults.

I believe that spiritual values and idealism—within or without organized religion—are as real and as powerful as the physical and intellectual attributes of human being.

I believe that we can give our children standards to live by and keep them from cynically accepting amorality and immorality, even though much of society as a whole may be corrupt and cynical.

Chapter Seven

The Roots of Idealism

I once heard a young teenager announce defiantly, "Sex is just a natural instinct that's meant to be enjoyed," as if that was all there was to it. That's like saying "The Taj Mahal is a structure to keep the rain out," or "Beethoven's Fifth symphony is sound waves."

Human sexuality is as broad and complex as a fine tapestry. In most other animal species, sexuality is simply an instinctive means of survival; for us, that is only the beginning. Our sexuality is related at the unconscious level, as psychoanalysis has shown, to other spiritual forces, such as the love between children and their parents, the spiritual devotion between husband and wife, compassion for those in trouble, dedication to leaders and causes, the creation and enjoyment of beauty, even the search for the secrets of nature and science.

That's quite a list. How do I justify it? Humans have been recording the evidence since the beginnings of time. The uniquely human quality of sexual response—the spiritual aspect—has inspired poets and dramatists, painters and sculptors, religious and cultural leaders. Sigmund Freud systemized it in his exploration of the unconscious minds of his patients and of the stages of the child's emotional development.

A Child's First Influences

Freud's analysis of human sexuality and emotional development has so permeated twentieth century Western thought that many people don't recognize its origin. To me it's an essential key to understanding human behavior and idealism.

Many of the feelings I am going to include are felt not at the conscious level but at the unconscious level. We've learned about them from the psychoanalysis of innumerable adults and children, as well as from direct observation. If some aspects of these feelings seem unlikely, even preposterous to us, it is because we tended to suppress and bury them at six or seven years of age in the transition to middle childhood. But many parents have reported these patterns to me about their children and I have seen them myself.

Between birth and three years, the human child undergoes a series of fundamental emotional developments. Before birth, babies are enveloped in the mother's womb, which protects them and supplies all their needs. That symbiotic, blissful relationship with the mother extends to newborn babies—they wake, are cuddled and fed, sleep, wake again, are cuddled and fed over and over again.

At about half a year babies instinctively start to assert a little independence. They want to hold onto things, including their bottles. Having learned to sit, they want to sit all the time and fight against being laid down for changing though it has to be done a dozen times a day. They become impatient with being hugged too much. But of course they are still helplessly dependent on the mother. She not only feeds and comforts, she gives and inspires love, she interprets the child's inner feelings: "There, there, Linda is hungry and Mommy will feed her." She interprets the outer world: "It's a doggie. The doggie is barking. He loves Linda." This behavior is universal in good human parents; it's more than just baby talk. The parent is slowly building in the child knowledge, trust and the ability to cope.

Independence Versus Dependence

The conflict between dependence and the need for independence, which will continue for twenty years, intensifies during the second and third years, making children often behave ambivalently. They are cooperative one minute and balky the next. This often makes life difficult for the parents.

By about three years children seem to feel sufficient independence to act more consistently positive toward their parents. Back at one and two they tried to imitate *some* of their parents actions. Now they want to be like them through and through, in feeling as well as actions—to identify with them fully. Boys and girls express it differently.

The boy, sensing that he is on the way to manhood, particularly admires his father, thinks him the most powerful, wise and richest man in the world, tries to walk like him, talk like him, take on his interests, and act out his occupation as well as he can understand it. He longs to grow up and be exactly like his father. With the help of a girl and a doll he "plays house," which means acting out the role of husband and father.

A boy identifies with his mother in certain respects too, though not nearly as broadly as with his father. He longs to have a baby to cherish, as he has been cherished. He wants to grow one in his abdomen, and may not accept the explanation that only girls can do that. He falls in love with his mother, who is by far the most important female in his life. He considers her the world's most attractive and accomplished woman. He is apt to announce that he wants to marry her some day. He is too inexperienced to realize that this is not appropriate. This intensified attachment to her will help to form his feminine ideal: some of her physical and emotional characteristics, and the kind of relationship she has had with her husband and him, will probably influence the kind of woman he will fall in love with and marry years later.

In a similar way, the girl child identifies strongly with her mother: she idolizes and emulates her, practicing the same activities. Her ambition is to grow up to be just like her. To a lesser extent she identifies with her father, perhaps in some of his interests. She falls in love with her father and he becomes her masculine ideal. She is eager to have a baby and she "plays house" endlessly with a boy and a doll.

At this age boys and girls are apt to become involved in sex play, in the sense of examining and touching their own genitals, and deciding to undress, inspect, and perhaps touch each other. The game of "playing doctor" serves the same purpose. Children now have an increasing interest in where babies come from.

Overestimating the Parents

Idealism and spiritual values are not the invention of religious leaders of past times or of moralists of today; they are an expression of biological human nature, just as real as hunger or fear. They are the means by which the achievements and aspirations of society have been carried over from generation to generation. Sometimes idealistic goals are highly advanced (as in the success of physicists in gradually unraveling the ultimate secrets of the universe). Sometimes they are lost, as in today's widespread cynicism about the meaning of human existence. In any case, the recognition that ideals and spiritual values are real and achievable is really the central purpose of this book.

I want to emphasize that children at age three to six don't just love, admire and identify with their parents—they *overestimate* them; they see them larger than life. In the child's eyes, the mother and father are incredibly attractive, rich, possessing almost magical powers, are able to make miracles, and lead a charmed life.

This view of their parents has two vital effects: It gives children an idealized overestimation of what they themselves can become and what they can accomplish in their own adult lives. If sustained by the parents' ideals and encouragement through the rest of childhood, it can lead them to high achievement later in life.

Conversely, if the parents lack vision and idealism, their children's aims will gradually shrink.

What puts an end to the idyllic dreams of children of three, four, and five years is an accumulation of anxieties, mainly at the unconscious levels of the mind. At about two and a half—if they have the opportunity to see each other's bodies—children become aware that girls do not have penises. Both boys *and* girls are likely to be disturbed by this, as we learn from doll play and drawings. Boys usually think some accident or operation has occurred and worry about a similar fate for themselves. The girl may assume that she has somehow lost her penis or that her mother thought so little of her that she failed to give her one. Girls tend to be more resentful than worried, because the worst has apparently happened already.

At three or four years, girls can dream of having their fathers as partners, as boys can dream of marrying their mothers. But gradually, by five, six and seven, they realize that their parents are already married and not available. This arouses some jealousy and hostility, mostly unconscious, although these feelings may break through and lead the child to show hostile behavior. In the boy, these feelings of rivalry tend to focus on his father's penis, so much larger than his own, and he feels an impulse to harm it. I remember well the half joking, half angry snatching motions one of my sons made toward my penis at this age.

The boy may assume that his father has harmful designs on him, not only because of the boy's hostile feelings but also because of his unconscious wish to have his father out of the way so he can monopolize his mother. The fear that his father might have hostile designs on his penis is reinforced by his assumption that boys can easily lose their penises, as girls seem to have done. This fits with the observation that both boys and girls are apt to have bad mutilation dreams at this age.

What convinces the child psychoanalyst that most children go through this phase, is observing children of four, five, six and seven at play therapy. They see children playing out these obsessions about hostile rivalry with parents and genital injury, by means of drawings, doll play and made-up stories. Children do not realize that they are revealing their own feelings in playing out these fantasies and by adulthood they have been forgotten or repressed. I myself have been convinced many times over that these fears and hostilities are real and usual.

Turning to Impersonal Interests

By six and seven these anxieties begin to squelch the boys' longing to monopolize his mother and to have babies. His interests turn with relief to impersonal matters, such as curiosity about nature and science and a desire to learn the three Rs. In those parts of the world that have schools, it has been sensed that children's curiosity about impersonal matters makes them ready and eager for organized academic work at about six or seven years.

Now children tranfer some of their identification with parents to identification with their peers, mainly of the same sex. The boy or girl of eight or nine groans loudly at a love scene in a movie or television show. The child no longer openly worships his father and mother or tries to be just like them. To emphasize the change, the child may cultivate bad table manners, sloppy personal appearance, rude language, unpleasant habits such as picking his or her nose or kicking the table leg at meals. Instead of showing so much admiration of parents, children discover new heroes in television and the comics.

Children at this age form secret clubs or gangs, admitting those of the same age who share their interests and ideals, excluding those who don't qualify. This is a way of sorting out and codifying their own standards, and it leads to a certain amount of intolerance and cliquishness. Children living without other children of the same age may invent imaginary companions and situations to satisfy the same kind of need. By adolescence, heroes and heroines are likely to range from sports and entertainment figures to real or fictional characters they know from books or television.

The pressure of the sex hormones at 11, 12 and 13 turns childrens' interest back again to romance, sex and intense personal feelings. But the inhibition of heterosexuality that has lasted from about six to twelve years may first direct some adolescents' adoration toward adults or peers of the same sex, in what are called crushes. Only later do these individuals get enough courage to fall in love with someone of the opposite sex, perhaps a movie or television star about whom the adolescent can fantasize various encounters without any risk of having to face the person in reality or of making blunders out of inexperience. Next may come an infatuation with a real adult teacher or neighbor, and finally a peer of the opposite sex.

At this stage, children become interested in other aspects of human relationships. They are keenly concerned with conflicts that arise in their daily lives—with friends, schoolmates, brothers and sisters, parents and teachers. They are forming patterns of belief and behavior, and they want to discuss rights and wrongs.

This is a good age for parents to encourage a little discussion of ethics and values, not by preaching or scolding but by friendly talk. Hearing a respected teacher or even a parent explaining his or her values reinforces the actual experiences children are having in their own lives. It is a time when issues take on real significance, as children begin to understand the effects of tolerance and intolerance, respect and disrespect, love and hate. It is also a time when they can learn to be tolerant of and appreciate religious beliefs, skin colors, customs that are different from their own—especially if respected teachers show the way.

Between nine and twelve years—before adolescent rebelliousness becomes hardened and before the teenage inclination to see the opinions of peers as the ultimate truth and parents' views as hopelessly out of date—is a good time for parents to discuss ideas and ideals with their children, including those concerning sex and marriage.

If a child comes home from school with news of a classmate accused of shoplifting, for example, it's helpful to discuss questions of personal rights, property rights, and the need for laws. If the child has seen or been part of a dispute or fight, it's educational to discuss what brought it about and what might have been done to avoid it.

When table talk turns to a teenage pregnancy in the neighborhood, parents can sound out their childrens' reactions and points of view. It's an opportunity to discuss such things as the possible interruption or end of education for the young parents, the baby's right to a regular family life, and whether sex is just a physical instinct or has a spiritual aspect.

A neighborhood divorce lets the parents wonder aloud about impulses and consequences: whether the couple knew each other well at the time of marriage, whether they realized that marriages don't last unless both parties are ready to make sacrifices, that couples have to learn to understand each other's feelings in order to get along harmoniously.

Family discussion needn't concentrate on negative, pessimistic concerns. Children should know that openly discussing real situations can take place in a friendly spirit, even when there is a difference of opinion or outright disagreement, as long as mutual respect is felt and shown. The assumption should always be that sharing ideas should be interesting, honest and helpful for the future.

The Emotional Tasks of Adolescence

There are several vital tasks to be accomplished in adolescence and youth. The first, of course, is to gain increasing emotional independence from parents. Achieving that independence, however, is often difficult and never complete. Most young people can gradually become independent without total rebellion, although there may be plenty of friction, disagreement and arguing for its own sake. Our society's need for prolonged education complicates the drive for independence, since children who are physically mature must often remain financially dependent for years.

The intensity of adolescent revolt is often greatest in the individuals who were most attached in childhood. Even rebels who storm out of the house in a fury, never to return, still carry their parents' influence with them. And children who adamantly reject their parents' values on a conscious level will be unconsciously bound by some of those values for life.

The second task of adolescence is to adjust to a new body, new feelings, new interests and aims, new friendships, and a deeper realization of their own identity. The sexual urge at puberty is overpowering enough to dominate all the other changes in feelings. Depending on the nature and strength of influences within and outside the family, the urge may soon lead to sexual experimentation and to intercourse. Or this may take years. Interestingly, the *Kinsey Report* showed that, on average, people with more education were slower to begin sexual experimentation.

The Conflicts of Sexuality

Adolescence has always been complicated by inner conflicts—young people torn between the need to achieve independence from parents and the fear of letting go, between newfound sexual desire and the strong taboos imposed back at six to nine years of age. While the basic problems are as old as our species, relaxed attitudes and technological progress have changed their expression and their solutions a lot in the last generation or so.

Probably no other aspect of life has changed as quickly and radically as have attitudes about sex—partly because of generally relaxed standards, partly because of sex education, partly because of impatience with censorship and partly because of more efficient contraception. Unlike their counterparts of just a few decades ago, today's adolescents enter puberty fully aware of—if not directly knowledgeable about—sexual feelings, sexual practices, and sexual preference. Subjects once clouded in mystery are wide open. Rising figures for teen pregnancy in the past 30 years and the fact that first intercourse is coming at progressively younger ages make clear that patterns have changed across all social and income groups.

This open attitude toward sexuality has undoubtedly helped to get rid of many foolish and downright dangerous notions that damaged the physical and emotional well being of many people in the past. Nevertheless, the pendulum has swung so far that sexuality is widely trivialized, despiritualized and coarsened, particularly in the popular media.

Sex education has generally focused on the physiology of sex, birth control, disease prevention, and undoing the fear and guilt about normal sexual behavior. All of this has been of great value. However, the difficulty many modern Americans have in talking about feelings in general, about sexual feelings in particular, about ideals, plus the constitutional taboo against teaching religion in schools, have meant that the vast, complex, rich field of spiritual aspects of sexuality have been left out, ignored. This is unfortunate.

It is good for young people to hear that some adolescents with high ideals have, throughout Western society and recorded history preferred to save full physical intimacy until marriage, or until they are at least considering marriage seriously. To point out that sex and marriage are as much spiritual as physical does not mean that the physical pleasure will be limited: it may in fact be enhanced. In cultures that postpone sexual intimacy until couples are committed to sharing their lives and aspirations, people may become passionate lovers for life. Such reassurance can strengthen those adolescents who feel unready for sexual activity despite pressure from their uninhibited classmates.

I believe that children in the preadolescent years as well as in adolescence want to and should know their parents' opinions, especially in these days when so much of their education comes from television, movies and advertisements, and when moral standards have been relaxed dramatically.

As they move toward adulthood, adolescents want the freedom to adopt their own standards. But they are generally eager to hear the views of contemporaries, older youths, teachers and entertainment idols about what to believe and how to conduct themselves.

They also really want to know their parents' beliefs about sex, marriage, careers, money, and ethics generally, but they usually won't admit it because they fear being bound by their parents' opinions. Recognizing their children's drive to become independent, parents have to be more tactful than others. It antagonizes youths when their parents express the attitude that their children should agree with them because they are older and know more about life. That kind of condescension is counterproductive because it convinces adolescents that their parents are dogmatic and out of date. Instead parents should discuss issues with their children just as they would with friends—listening attentively to their views, not contradicting, perhaps not even expressing their own views until they have heard the children out.

I believe that when discussing sex and marriage, parents should *always* include the spiritual and idealistic aspects. They should take care not to preach or lecture. If they give their own views as beliefs, not dogma, children have room to respond from their own perspectives. If adolescents keep arguing back, it's better for the parent to say, "I see what you mean," and go on to another subject. Continuing arguments and counter-arguments only harden positions on both sides. Adolescents are more likely to consider adult views if they can think them over alone or discuss them amongst themselves.

Parents need to realize that even after their children's sexual urges becomes strong enough to overcome their inhibitions—whether that happens at 15 or at 25—the sublimated, idealized, spiritual portion of the sexual drive remains.

When a young person "falls madly in love," I believe, like Freud, that the suddenness, the specificity, the intensity, and the quality of mystery in the relationship is in part a revival of the young child's adoration and overidealization of the parent of the opposite sex.

This revival is likely to occur because the adolescent lover is unconsciously inspired by some similarity of parental character or appearance in the beloved. It happens in adolescence and adulthood because the adoration of the parent had to be given up and suppressed at six or seven years. If there is not some special significance like this, why does a youth fall in love with one individual, not with all reasonably attractive people? Psychoanalysis of individuals reveals the connection. So does the old popular song "I Want A Girl Just Like The Girl Who Married Dear Old Dad."

The yearning of teenagers idealizes and overestimates qualities of the beloved, they daydream about great deeds and achievements in the services of the beloved. I remember constant daydreams about rescuing my first love from a burning city in a powerful sports car, at the age of 13. Falling in love keeps being repeated until experience and maturity outweigh unrealistic infatuation. If an ideal marriage follows, it is partly because of the strength of the idealism inspired at the age of three and four.

Chapter Eight

Instilling Values

The idea that spiritual values are for poets and clergymen, while people in business and industry are meant to be preoccupied only with profits, is intensely corruptive, but has had a new wave of popularity. It's a fairly frequent attitude on Wall Street where real emotional contact with customers is minimal and money is often considered the only reality.

Our nation has had its share of robber barons, but it has also had far-sighted individuals who saw fit to reinvest the profits from their financial successes in improving the social fabric. One was Andrew Carnegie, who in the last century used the large profits from his iron and steel businesses to establish free public libraries. Many of our great universities, museums and medical centers were built by people who willingly returned their wealth to society. Some of the brilliant young people who have led the way in developing computer information systems are reinvesting some of their time, talent and money to bring social benefits to the nation.

Drama, literature, television, comics and movies sometimes give us examples of how wrongdoers get exposed and punished. Unfortunately, however, the scoundrels are often the more fascinating characters. It's more constructive for children to know how the people who demonstrate high performance and high principles are admired and even loved, even though their stories may not be as gripping. The considerate factory owner or office manager can be an important role model for aspiring young people about to enter business.

I want to further discuss values, particularly spiritual and idealistic ones. To some people these mean some form of religious beliefs. To be sure, these beliefs, if strongly held, are potent spiritual beliefs. But atheists and agnostics also can have strong spiritual beliefs. I want to emphasize non-religious spiritual values. By spiritual values I mean any qualities or values that are simply not materialistic—not love of money or other possessions, although I appreciate and enjoy both, or love of power, which I enjoy too, but suspect.

To me, spiritual values include the dependent love children have for their parents, parent's love for their children, and our love for people who show kindness. Spiritual values mean loyalty to friends and relatives, dedication to causes and country, kindness to those in need, bravery and persistence, creativity and appreciation of the arts. For those who adhere to a religion, it includes reverence for God.

I believe that the capacity for spiritual values is inborn, instinctual in children. Values are expressed as children adore, over-estimate, imitate, and strive to be like their parents who love them, especially in the years between three and six. They see their parents as larger than life—more beautiful, wiser, richer, more powerful and more skillful than they are in reality.

This overestimating of parental qualities is a biological instinct developed through evolution. In other animals, the drive is more limited, but easier to recognize. When we see wild birds and animals or household pets imitating their parents' behavior, we recognize it as a basic means for survival from one generation to the next. It's the same in humans.

As children pull back from their parents in the six to ten year phase, and as adolescents become more independent, the intense adoration of parents is transformed or sublimated into more distant loves—sports or entertainment heroes, great figures from history and science, and creators of music, poetry, and the other arts.

To keep those kinds of spiritual values and ideals alive and vigorous during childhood, adolescence and youth, it is necessary that at least one parent share their children's idealism about the world and their potential for carrying the world forward. If neither parent believes in or speaks about spiritual values, the child's values gradually shift to a more mundane level, especially in the adolescent years when skepticism and cynicism about parental beliefs tend to be high.

Where Do Spiritual Values Belong?

In an industrialized or post-industrial world, where everything is rationalized and subject to analysis and criticism, many people wonder where there is a place for the kind of spiritual and idealistic values I am talking about. I believe if they belong anywhere, they belong everywhere; the dearth of them is the main cause of the sickness of our society.

Ideally, spiritual values belong in marriage, so husband and wife will revere and cherish each other. That ideal is rooted in their own childhoods when they adored and overidealized *their* own parents. Spiritual values also belong in the respect idealistic parents show for their children—nurturing, counseling and inspiring them.

Children who grow up with a strong sense of idealism will have respected and loved their parents. As they mature, they will show love and respect also for their teachers and friends. In adulthood they will be ready to start another loving, idealizing cycle with spouses and children of their own. They will be disposed to deal in a friendly, trusting spirit with fellow workers, who will tend to return the response in kind. In their business and community lives they will respect and treat their customers, clients and colleagues with consideration and warmth.

Spiritual values—in the form of honesty, fair dealing, respect for subordinates, superiors and the public—should dominate the relationships and the manner in which businesses and governments are run.

If we expect the next generation to continue the high ideals our society professes, its leaders must believe in and live by those ideals. I feel particularly bitter about our government officials using the excuse of "national security" to deceive the public, break laws and defy the

Constitution. Although such actions may seem to achieve the government's purpose at the moment, they destroy its credibility and effectiveness and make cynics of millions of citizens.

Cynics would have us believe there is no realistic basis for believing in any motivation beyond materialism. It is true that the human species has the capacity for greed, suspicion, hatred and cruelty. But I believe that most human beings possess a stronger capability for spiritual values.

Whether or not those values are embodied in religion or in a humanistic philosophy does not matter as much as whether these universal values are maintained and strengthened in the face of new and ever more insidious challenges.

Transmitting and Reinforcing Values

The child's drive to take on the values they see in their parents is part of a long process of evolution to ensure that the young learn the best of what their parents have to offer. That drive is inspired and recharged in each generation, assuring us of a continuing source of spiritual energy that will foster the nobler, kindlier aspects of humanity, in spite of the greed and hatred that exist.

Maintaining spiritual values through childhood and adolescence depends on their being reinforced and made specific by the teachings of parents, teachers, religious and political leaders. This teaching needs to be positive and realistic, not disapproving or threatening, and is best delivered by example, not by preaching.

The opportunities are everywhere—in discussions and comments about friendship and marriage, education and jobs, national and international events, scientific developments and artistic accomplishments. Only when cynicism takes over, when parents and teachers don't have anything positive to say, when leaders lack vision, is the potentiality for high aspirations and idealism lost for the next generation.

Can Idealistic Values Survive?

The most destructive forces in the industrialized world today are fanatical competitiveness, unbalanced materialism, and the unbridled ambition for income and prestige in a person's occupation. I don't mean that any of these drives are evil in themselves, but together and unbalanced by idealism, they are making people's lives ever more stressful, more devoid of spiritual meaning, and more demoralized.

This deadly combination of excessive competitiveness, materialism and ambition relegates genuine human relationships to a low priority. It makes us slaves rather than creators in our work. It erodes marriages. It makes jobs more important than children. It takes the joy out of child care and leaves only the irritations. The tensions it generates make us more aggressive and less loving. It leaves us unfulfilled—at the end of the day and at the end of our lives.

I believe strongly in the evolutionary, psycho-biological basis for the idealism that has allowed the human race to go as far as it has gone. I now realize the truth of the Biblical declaration, "Man cannot live by bread alone." Otherwise why would human beings be able to create such inspiring literature, drama, art and architecture or to celebrate the beauty of life in poetry, music and dance or to better human existence through advances in science and technology?

PART THREE:
Creating a Better World

Chapter Nine

Toward a Better World

To create a better world for our children, we must first raise our children to be kind and caring: creating a better person will help make the world a better place. Children are, of course, an integral part of the family.

The family alone cannot make a better world. We must change our communities and workplaces to be more family-oriented. To do this our citizens must get more involved in schools and politics. One of the reasons for the sad state of America is that our citizens have been apathetic for far too long.

Strengthening the Family

The most crucial area for making a better world is in rearing our children. I believe that we should not raise them with the major aim of getting ahead in the world financially, as many are raised today. Instead, they should be reared from the age of two through adolescence with the ideals of helpfulness, kindliness and service to others, whether they eventually choose to work in a helping profession, business or industry. Parents can't expect to engender this attitude by preaching, scolding or nagging. They must set examples, treating each other and their children with respect and expecting their respect in return. For children dearly love to be grown up and to be helpful, if their efforts are appreciated.

One of the striking phenomena of this century is a growing acceptance of sexual role-reversal in the home and workplace. It is becoming more common for husbands and wives to share (not necessarily equally) household chores and responsibilities. Paternal leave from a job when a new child is born is becoming almost as accepted as maternal leave. These trends would have been unthinkable even a few generations ago, and if they occurred at all the male would have been branded as henpecked and the woman a misfit.

To the extent that this trend emphasizes the importance of home and family, it is for the good. Yet in a justifiable demand for equality with men, women can now compete as fanatically in the workplace as many men do. And with the freedom to join the rat race, some women are now sharing with men the rat-race diseases—stress, tension, and the tendency to put personal success above feelings and concern for others. This effect, in men or women, is inevitably transferred to their children and families. Too bad more men can't reverse *their* traditional roles and learn something from women, with their instinctive realization that family, feelings and friendships are the richest and longest lasting rewards in life.

Strengthening our Schools

Schools and educators can play a powerful role, second only to the influence of parents in forming children's attitudes and values. Yet to a great extent our schools are failing us. More and more children are dropping out of high school, and many that graduate are unequipped for the available jobs. To meet the challenge of producing useful citizens for a new century, I believe we need radical reform of education, starting with curriculums that emphasize practical skills for solving real problems, yet instill an understanding and appreciation for creativity, imagination, and beauty.

Old-fashioned traditions and methods simply aren't working in a society that has changed as much as ours has in this century. Yet we know that some schools engage children's interest and enthusiasm, encouraging initiative, problem solving, cooperation and creativity.

I urge schools and universities to stop judging students solely on their grades—to do away with the conventional grading system altogether. The drive to achieve high scores distorts the real purpose of education. Children are pressured into acquiring arbitrary letter or number grades and high scores on competitive tests, but this approach turns many of them away from learning about the world and how to function in it. This quest for measurable achievement instead of the joy of learning puts undue stress on many children and may convince marginal students—who need the most guidance and encouragement—to drop out.

Just as grades in schools are a form of competition that can be destructive, physical punishment teaches children that violence is appropriate and contributes to the proliferation of violence in society. Humiliation is equally wrong as a punishment, teaching children that criticism and put-downs of others are acceptable retaliation for their own dissatisfactions. It is not wise to compare one child with another, either at home or in school, but to accept each one as she or he is, in temperament and appearance.

I also recommend a vast overhaul of the way we prepare young people for working in a changing world. We need a massive shift to new kinds of apprenticeship programs, designed specifically for a society where manual labor is rapidly being replaced by service and interpersonal jobs. When students work part-time and attend school part-time, they see the practical connections between acquiring knowledge and using it in the real world. Learning by doing is the best way to improve skills and to keep children who are not motivated toward serious academic work from dropping out. Apprenticeship programs also get businesses involved in their communities and in educating the workforce alongside the public schools.

Strengthening Jobs and Communities

As children go out into the world, they are influenced by schools, businesses and government. As a former medical school professor, I have seen how medical students and medical schools can better serve their communities by closer involvement with them at the start of their careers. The same concept can be effective in other occupations and professions, by detaching students, interns and apprentices from the purely theoretical aspects of their work and mating them with the community at large.

Such outreach programs are essential, not just to help business, unions, schools and government work more effectively but to emphasize the importance of involving people with people. The purpose, of course, is to let young people know that all human endeavor takes place on a two-way street—that we all interact at some level of our lives, that the most beneficial interactions are those that reward all parties in a fair way, and we gain by giving, not just by receiving. By making trades and professions truly responsive to those they serve, we can effectively combat many of the social and economic ills that weaken our society.

Citizen Participation

Another broad area in which we must change our present pattern is by increasing greatly our political activity. I point out the embarrassing fact that in our democracy only half of our citizens bother to vote, which turns our government over to the special interests. One possible factor is the cynical belief that the two major party platforms are often indistinguishable. Another is the mistaken American belief that the satisfaction of all our needs can be achieved only by individual competitive effort, not through politics or other collective effort.

Voting discriminately, in primaries and in the final election, is crucial. After officials are installed, citizens as individuals and in groups must watch their voting records, lobby them, write them letters and if necessary, picket and demonstrate. Citizen activism keeps politicians on their toes and lets them know that people are looking over their shoulders. The 1980s and early 1990s were a period when greed was in vogue and politicians were out of touch. I believe that we can once again make citizen participation the rule rather than the exception and community involvement popular. With popular support, a president and Congress can make improvements in education, job training and health care and help turn this country around.

I believe that the key to a better world for our children—and ourselves—is to reassert the importance of values and to encourage idealism.

Chapter Ten

Better Families

Some people believe that the American family is dying because of skyrocketing divorce, the increase in parents working far from home and the feeling that jobs demand more attention than the children. Because of grossly inadequate high-quality day care and the impact and influence of amoral and immoral television programs, the family has lost its dominant role. In addition to these trends that have a particular impact on children, there are the general trends that are corrupting the whole society—excessive competition and materialism, the shocking amount of violence that younger and younger children are participating in, the coarsening and despiritualization of society.

But I think that it's too soon to count the family out. The essence of the family is the relationship between the spouses, and between at least one parent and the children. The latter is, on the average, the stronger bond, harder to break, because it's the core of every child's instinctual existence. The parents can adjust, for example, to the disruptions of divorce, but children go on begging the parents to get back together for years. And they carry the image, the imprint of their parents' characters, for the rest of their lives.

As a pediatrician I've been impressed that when parents are visibly respectful and loving toward each other and toward their children, the children—most of the time—are kind to each other and naturally helpful and polite toward their parents.

Spirituality in the Family

A first step in getting spirituality, love and kindliness back into the family is to cultivate them in the marriage. Some parents need to be more aware of the atmosphere they create between themselves and their spouses and between themselves and their children. A time to observe these relationships is when they first get home from work. Do they get a friendly response or does the rest of the family turn glum? Few people realize that they themselves have the power to evoke one response or the other: a hug or a loving greeting may be enough to initiate a good mood. Instead they may fall into a passive attitude in which they assume they have no defense against a disagreeable spouse and have only one choice—to snarl back. Five minutes of masterfulness on first stepping inside the front door may be more productive than it is a half hour later when the fat is in the fire.

One factor in children who are quarrelsome with each other and less than cooperative with parents, may be chronic impatience in the parents that rubs the children the wrong way. If so, it is wise for the parents to cultivate serenity, perhaps with meditation or counseling.

Religion as a Binder of Families

It used to be that most children in America grew up within their family's religion. They stayed with it and passed it on to *their* children. This holding to a family religious tradition is still common but not nearly as much so as before.

I feel that the children and adults in families that adhere to a specific religion (as I don't) or a firm set of moral standards (as I do) are fortunate. Most human beings, by their nature, want to live by some set of spiritual beliefs, whether or not they are part of a formal religion.

That's why most societies around the world have established religions, based on more or less similar moral precepts. It gives people's lives a firm, comforting framework. It explains the mysteries of Nature. It tells people clearly, what their God and their fellow human beings expect of them, what the rewards are for obedience and what the punishments are for disobedience. Religious leaders interpret the details and the applications of the major beliefs, but the principles remain universal.

At the opposite extreme from the believers are the firm atheists, people who have turned against the family's religion, if any, and against all other religions. Such rejection is typically a part of adolescent rebellion, but is often on the basis of a single, pivotal experience, and sometimes on the basis of what non-believers feel to be pure, rational thought. They will pass their disbelief to their children, most of whom will accept disbelief, at least until adolescence.

There are many people who are in between, not only the agnostics who wonder a lot but the non-believers who are simply not interested for themselves but are concerned with how they should present religion to their children in a country where so many are churchgoers. They fret, for example, about whether they can send them to Sunday school or Hebrew school if they themselves don't attend church or temple.

There are those who assume that there is a creator but see no basis for believing that the creator is like a person or, specifically, like the Jehovah of the Old Testament. There are those who admire some of Christ's teachings, but don't feel an obligation to believe all of them in the way that I agree with his belief in the extreme importance of love.

The main cause of the skepticism and confusion about religion today is that the sciences have contradicted most of the specific stories of the Bible. The story of creation in the Book of Genesis is the prime example. Many people are able to accept Genesis not as God's decree but as the plausible guess of religious leaders thousands of years ago about how the world might have begun. And they may accept some of the spiritual messages of the Bible.

Today, many young parents are rejecting the religion of their parents, while others raised with little or no religion now feel that they missed it and want to give their children some kind of religious training.

Is it fair for parents who don't attend church to require their children to go to religious schools? This is a question that seems to bother a lot of parents. After all, parents and society don't give children a choice about attending regular school. I suggest that parents who feel positive about the value of Sunday school send their children matter-of-factly, without asking them, from the age of three to six when children are not highly opinionated about such matters, especially if their friends attend. After age six the parents should discuss attendance with the children and arrive at a consensus. Then parents can let their children decide in the teen years.

I envy adult believers and their children for two reasons. First it gives them a moral and spiritual framework to support and inspire them—at least until the children get to late adolescence or early adulthood when they may want to rethink their religious or spiritual beliefs. The second reason is more cultural. It is good for children to get a sense of the background from which they have sprung—including the religious one, so that they will understand what their relatives and friends are talking about.

When children begin to study history and find that their ancestors belonged to this or that wave of immigrants to America, it makes them feel proud. To find where "the old country" is on a map of Europe, Africa, Latin America or Asia and learn what some of its history is, connects them with the rest of the world and with the past.

In a similar way, millions learn Bible stories in Sunday school, sing traditional hymns and recognize Biblical allusions in the arts. This knowledge broadens and enriches children's minds, making them feel they are part of the world, part of civilization.

Making High Tech Work for Families

If I have been critical of certain high-technology products—headset tape players, boom-box radios, video games and cable television—it's not for what they are but for some of the messages they communicate. I applaud the availability of information, educational material and performance art that would otherwise be unavailable to masses of young people. But I deplore the fact that the people who produce popular music, television programming, and video games exploit young people's senses and sensibilities with material that exalts disrespect, cruelty, coarse sex and materialism. I realize that not all children are vulnerable to such assaults, but too many are. Worse yet, neither broadcasters nor parents can truly insulate children from the more insidious material once it is sold or broadcast.

Nonetheless, the development of electronics has revolutionized the way humans calculate, store, retrieve and communicate information. Technology has affected our lives in hundreds of other ways, from hand held household gadgets to scientific wizardry in the laboratory. Word processors, computer networks and facsimile machines have opened up new opportunities to teach, learn and interact—and young people are the quickest to understand and exploit these technological wonders.

In fact, some kinds of technology really can help to improve family values. The telephone, of course, is a tool that children now learn to use at an early age, and nothing is more convenient or enjoyable than letting children stay in touch with distant grandparents and relatives by the occasional telephone call. There comes a time, however, when limits may have to be placed on young people who use the phone incessantly to converse with friends. Once again, the best way to influence a child's telephone use is by example, which for many parents may not be the easiest thing to control themselves.

The telephone answering machine is another piece of technology that can be a blessing or a bother, depending on how children use it. For parents and children on the go, the ability to leave messages next to the home telephone is a real boon.

Even a video cassette recorder can help in a small way to preserve family values by shifting television programs to more convenient times for parents and children. If the evening news airs in the middle of the family dinner, you can easily tape and watch it after you put young children to bed. The same goes for children's programming; if a favorite show interferes with homework during the week, you can tape it for them to watch at a more convenient time.

Substitutes for Parental Care

The preferable situation for family well-being is the traditional one: two caring parents able to provide their children with shelter, nourishment and most importantly, love and security. While it's important for both parents to provide care, it is particularly desirable for one or the other to have plenty of time with infants and small children in the first two to three years, not simply to feed, clothe and keep them clean, but to give them a sense of security and intimacy with the parents. If the family's economic situation permits, it is better for one parent not to work outside the home during this period. If doing so is impossible financially, parents deserve incentives like short-term tax breaks or flexible work rules to stay with their children during these critical first years.

The problem is particularly hard for single mothers or single fathers faced with a choice of welfare dependency or poverty without some form of outside help. If support from an extended family is available—parents or a close relative in the household or nearby—the single parent can be a breadwinner and still be confident that his or her children are cared for and loved. Without that close support, the alternative is outside day care.

More and Better Day Care

The economic reality of two working parents is not going away, nor are the inherent problems of combining work and family life. The solution is not to try to turn back the clock. For some, full-time, carefully chosen baby sitters meet the need for child care. For others the "information highway" is letting more people work at home. Another answer is to provide care for preschool children at or near the workplace during the work day. For example, the city of San Francisco requires day-care facilities to be included in all new office buildings.[1] Day-care centers are common all over America. Some municipalities are starting to offer day care as an adjunct to public schools. But parents must demand these through organized political activity.

We know that ideal day care, with carefully selected and trained teachers, and small groups, can produce children capable of close attachments and deep feelings. At the other extreme, we know that different care with large groups of children can produce shallow development.

Parents considering day care should visit those available, for several hours and several times, to see the quality of the care. The number of children for each teacher or assistant should not be greater than two more than the age of the children. For example, there should be no more than five three-year-olds per adult. A good teacher is not a drill sergeant. He or she watches the group and goes to the rescue of any child who is frustrated in his play or being bullied by another child.

Providers of day care should be trained and licensed, just as teachers have to be. Even more important is for them to have a loving, kindly attitude toward children and understand how the care-giving relationship can significantly shape the child's development. The child must know that he or she is with people who give the same kind of care and protection that parents do. Parents should have the assurance that their child is receiving responsible, concerned care every day, with kindliness and relaxed good humor.

Step Parenting

I found being a stepfather at age 72 the most difficult relationship of my life. My two sons were well into adulthood when my stepdaughter, an only child, was 11. Her parents had had an unhappy marriage and divorce. Ginger had her mother pretty much to herself from the age of seven, when her parents were divorced, until age 11 when I entered the picture.

Ginger wanted to stay loyal to both of her parents. Mary, her mother, had a job that included being out with professional people, but otherwise spent most her time with Ginger. I came on the scene for a workshop and Mary and I promptly fell in love. I returned to my apartment across the continent, but we continued our relationship by telephone. The point of all this detail is that we didn't give Ginger any chance to feel she was in on the choice of a stepfather. But that's not the whole explanation for her rejection of me. Millions of step-parents have been rejected whose stepchildren were acquainted and consulted from the start.

Ginger totally ignored me for years. She brushed past me when she came home from school and never answered my greetings. She never thanked me when she missed the bus and I drove her to school. On one of those occasions she allowed herself to ask, in a scornful tone, "Do you always drive this slowly?"

Mary and I consulted a psychiatric social worker who specialized in stepfamily problems. She comforted me somewhat by saying, "If you thought you could be accepted in a couple of years you were living in a fool's paradise." As a result of the consultation I became more patient, and Ginger and I made a gradual peace.

I was also reassured that my advanced age didn't make me automatically unpleasant to a pre-teenager when one of Ginger's friends, who we'd invited for two weeks on a boat trip, regularly called me "Benjy Boy."

I'd written an article years before on overcoming the difficulties of stepparenting in which I emphasized that they shouldn't try to be disciplinarians. Good advice. Theoretically! But I found that I got so angry at Ginger's rudeness to me, as well as her silent defiance of her mother's rules about such matters as wearing her braces from the end of school in the afternoon to the end of breakfast the next day, that I couldn't possibly refrain from interfering—not that I ever succeeded. My anger prevented me from following my own advice.

Why couldn't we get counseling for Ginger? We tried, but she rejected it indignantly. "There's nothing the matter with *me*!" she would say.

I am writing about this for several reasons. First, I do not know all the answers to family problems, and I believe that all of us can gain by getting counseling. Even though I give advice in these matters, no one can be his or her own therapist—everyone needs an objective outside opinion.

Second, relationships with stepchildren can be exceedingly difficult to develop and stepparents must be infinitely patient. Patience and time are great healers. Keep the channels of communication open and eventually the stepchild will begin to open up. Ginger and I eventually became close friends. She encouraged her school to invite me to address her graduating class—and I did. When she married in 1989, I walked her down the aisle.

After Ginger graduated from high school we were asked to write companion pieces for *Redbook* magazine about problems between stepfathers and stepchildren. Ginger emplasized how close she and her mother were after the divorce and what a shock it was when I entered the picture. She feared losing her mother and felt abandoned when Mary and I went off on a trip together. One event that stuck in her mind as a turning point in our relationship is when I sided with Ginger against her mother during an argument.

In retrospect, it is clear that no matter how much I was suffering, Ginger suffered more. I should have examined the relationship from her perspective, but I failed to at the time. The burden on improving these sensitive relationships must be on the stepparent. It is the stepparent who should have the maturity, objectivity and patience to make the relationship work. And it is the stepparent who is the "intruder."

In the 18 years that I have been in the family, my relationship with Ginger has very gradually improved. Now we are good and affectionate friends. But it took a great deal of time and patience to reach this result.

Counseling does not always work, but it rarely hurts to try seeking professional advice. Not everyone can afford to pay for therapy, but usually it can be obtained for a modest cost. Some therapists charge for their services on a sliding scale, based on income. Sometimes health insurance will pay for part or all of the cost. It may be helpful to consult with a priest, rabbi or other clergyman. Often a close friend or relative can be helpful in working out problems.

Schools often have counselors for children to talk with. Many schools, because divorce is now so prevalent, often form groups to discuss problems with children of divorce.

Aids to Family Solidarity

Every family develops its own patterns and character. I suggest the following as twelve ways to build strong, positive family values.

Family Meals

Eat together as often as possible, certainly several full family dinners a week. Involve everyone: young children can set the table and older ones can clear up. Share lots of conversation, but avoid criticism or scolding at mealtimes.

Family Meetings

Hold weekly gatherings to plan family activities, trips and vacations and discuss both immediate and persistent problems. Share with each other schedules, plans, problems and accomplishments, likes and dislikes. Everyone has an agenda item and children's opinions count.

Quiet Time

Schedule daily stress-reduction periods when the whole household is quiet. No television, record players, or loud activity. Find a form that suits your family: reading, meditation, prayer, exercise, yoga, massage, or whatever works for your family.

Community Service

Volunteer time and talent to worthy causes, with parents setting the model for children: hospital or clinic work, transportation or care for the elderly, meals-on-wheels, service on church committees, helping the homeless, other community or public service activities.

Participate in School

Tutor younger children if they fall behind. Become involved with children's teachers and administrators, to understand and to influence school policy. Participate in PTA. Help with after-school or summer-vacation activities, assist with clubs, coach teams, organize teen activities.

Family Recreation

Take regular family walks, hikes, bike rides or other activities that adults and children can enjoy together, either spontaneous or planned. Show children that recreation is important for all ages, not just for the young.

Make or Build Things Together

Share creative activities that have tangible results, such as cooking, sewing, music, kitchen-table crafts and science projects, toy making and model building. Let children take the lead, and go for accomplishment, not perfection.

Family Outings

Share organized trips to local fairs, sporting events, picnics, the circus, concerts and performance art, fishing trips or other activities that the family enjoys doing together. Give equal time for everyone's interests without excluding anyone.

Bring Children to Work

With the employer's cooperation, let children see the other part of adult life away from home. Explain your skills and knowledge, the equipment you use, your responsibilities and the end result of useful work.

Family Vacations

At least once a year, travel away from home so everyone can relax and have a good time. Discuss vacation ideas with children, let them know what to expect, and give older children a voice in making vacation plans in advance.

Limited Television

Watch television with children, monitor what they watch, and discuss what they see, at home and at friends' houses. As children mature, set mutually agreed limits on times and types of programming.

Staying Involved

Keep informed about community and national issues that affect your children. Become involved in the causes that matter to you. Write newspaper editors, participate in committee meetings, and join policy groups. Vote regularly, and take your child along to see how it's done. Run for office. Let children know your concerns and opinions, and listen to theirs.

Chapter Eleven

Raising Children to Be Kind

Our greatest hope for a better world and the best antidote for today's cynicism, I believe, is to bring up children inspired by their opportunities for being helpful and loving. We should not let them grow up believing that they are in the world primarily to acquire possessions or to get ahead. For if we give them no spiritual values to live by, they are wide open to the materialism pounded in by television programs, music videos and other commercial hucksterism.

Parents can set the example by not overemphasizing their jobs at the expense of families. Many children, while proud of their parents' important jobs, are bitter about the small amount of time spent with them.

By age two or three a child watches his parents carefully and wants to imitate every action. He wants to set the table, for instance: it's partly imitation but it's also kindness. A parent may miss the chance to show appreciation if he or she is afraid the plate may be broken and decide that it is easier and faster to do the job himself. Here is an opportunity to let the child set the spoons and forks, which can't be broken. By complimenting him and giving him the job of having his usefulness appreciated, the child gains confidence and self-esteem. A parent can also appeal to the child's striving to grow up by holding out the promise that pretty soon he will be able to set the plates too. Then the glasses. Later in childhood, children help clean and vacuum their rooms, make their beds and cook simple dishes for the family.

Instead of buying cards for birthdays and holidays, children by the age of three can make them—for parents and siblings, grandparents, aunts, uncles, cousins and friends. Later in childhood they can make simple gifts such as bead necklaces and solid wood airplane models. There are enough people and enough occasions to remind children throughout the year that they have the power to please others—and that it's just as exciting to give as it is to receive. The same goes for making decorations for the Christmas tree and helping to choose the favors for the birthday party. Children also enjoy knowing that toys can be repaired and given to younger children or to others through charitable organizations.

Maintaining Helpfulness

A crucial aspect of these expressions of concern, generosity, and love is how they are introduced and how they are maintained. The best way is when the child volunteers spontaneously, out of love or because the school or family has a tradition that appeals to the child. Some of the value is lost if the parents or the school *require* the service.

There is as well a growing sentiment in favor of a national or school-district requirement of community service at some point during high school, in order to connect the students with the community and make them more sensitive to the human problems there. I agree about the value of community service or participation at the high school—and also at the college—levels. But part of the value is lost if the service is simply a bureaucratic requirement rather than partly springing from the students' desire to understand other people's problems and to help them.

There are a variety of community services that could use adolescents' help, provided there is thoughtful supervision and provided the institution is willing to make this contribution. An example would be the non-technical chores in a hospital, such as guiding the bookmobile, tutoring children or reading to them in a children's institution. Interestingly, it has been discovered that when an adolescent who is behind in reading tutors a young child who has the same problem, the reading scores of both will improve—they are "reading buddies."

In order to meet two demands, a day-care center can be set up in a high school to serve preschool children of the neighborhood or children of the high school faculty. Thus, at the same time providing a vital need for the community and their children, the high school students learn child care, child development and human relations in a dramatic way.

In relation to any of these "extra-curricular"activities, I think it is essential that the students meet once a week, individually or as a group, with a social studies teacher or a staff member of the institution to discuss their experiences, feelings—of frustration or success—and their conclusions, to be sure that they are coming to fresh understandings, not just intensifying old prejudices.

Then there is what we might call second-hand participation in the community in which a social worker is asked to read aloud a case report of a troubled family or takes a small group of students to a court hearing. I suggest the words "second-hand" because the high school students do not deal directly with the troubled individuals, but hear about someone else's dealings.

Adolescents can be encouraged to do volunteer work for causes—charitable, environmental, educational, political—including participating in election campaigns if they have a definite preference about candidates and issues.

But even if the child, whether at three or 16, truly volunteers, a minor crisis often occurs when the novelty wears off and the child ceases to volunteer. This is less likely to happen if the parent has had a very warm, uncritical relationship with the child all along, and if the parent has *daily* expressed appreciation of the child's help. But if the volunteering does cease, I think it is crucial that the parent not turn cross, but sit down with the child and explain in a loving way what a help the child's contribution has been and why the parent therefore asks the child to continue. This kind of serious but affectionate appeal is hard for a child to turn down.

Though I'm against parental preaching and scolding (I was scolded too much in my childhood), I'm strongly in favor of parents talking with their children about their own beliefs, their ideals—as long as it is done in a friendly, non-condescending way.

Too Many Gifts

Most American parents (including me) give all the gifts their children ask for, whether or not they are sensible, whether or not they can really afford all of them. It expresses their delight in their children, and that is good. But telling the department store Santa Claus every plaything they want and then having a frenzy of opening the presents on Christmas morning encourages a selfish and greedy attitude.

I think it would be better as the holidays approach for the parents to steer some of the talk to the opportunity for making simple presents or greeting cards for relatives and friends. That fosters the children's spirituality and is closer to the meaning of a religious holiday. Actually, children fall readily into the attitude that it's as blessed to give as to receive. I remember well my joy in making for my parents, in school, a stack of three small blotters tied with a ribbon. Adults needed blotters in 1910 because the ink in pens dried slowly. On the top blotter I glued a calendar and a picture I had drawn of a house with a winding path leading up to it and a winding wisp of smoke coming out of the chimney. And I remember my wild impatience waiting for my parents to unwrap my gift. I'm not implying that giving takes the place of receiving, only that giving should be equally important. Greediness shouldn't be whipped up by parents in their asking for lists of all the presents wanted or taking their children to the department store to tell Santa the same thing.

Reciprocity

Babies are born with the capacity to enjoy the love their parents show them. Three-month-olds squirm and twist their bodies with delight when their parents lean close, smile with adoration and give them exaggerated compliments. Before long the baby is smiling back, eyes sparkling, when a parent comes close. Babies who do not experience regular expressions of love don't smile or sparkle.

Babies want to reciprocate in their own ways. Parents see the beginnings of generosity when a year-old baby holds out a saliva-softened crust of bread to taste. After sizing up a house guest for 15 minutes, the infant may offer the adult one of the child's favorite playthings, even though he or she continues to hold onto it.

But more important than special occasions are the everyday opportunities to be helpful, considerate, polite and kind. How will children learn these attitudes? Not by being scolded. They learn primarily by the parents' example: how parents treat each other and their children.

As a pediatrician I've been impressed that when parents are genuinely respectful and loving toward each other and children, the children—most of the time—are generally kind to each other and naturally helpful and polite toward their parents. The reason a majority of our children are often quarrelsome with each other and less than cooperative with adults is that their parents are often irritable with them and expect the worst.

If parents are fortunate enough to be on good terms with their children most of the time, it's wise for them not to imply that kindliness is the only acceptable attitude in a good family. That forces children to suppress or deny their own hostility when they feel it; that suppression may lead to artificial, insincere sweetness. An occasional outburst of jealousy or rudeness may be shocking, but it's natural enough in the best of families.

To become secure, happy, productive adults, children need to develop such basic spiritual qualities as love, honesty, generosity, kindness, cooperation, idealism and an appreciation for beauty.

Because children consciously or unconsciously reflect their parent's habits and attitudes, the best way for parents to instill these values is by example. Parents who are positive influences on their children early in life give them values that last a lifetime.

Violence and Loveless Sex

We know for a fact now that watching violence on television or in movies gradually decreases the sense of horror of children and adults, that is, it has a desensitizing, brutalizing effect, not enough to turn a sensitively raised child into a criminal but enough to encourage murderousness in those reared without much love. We know that murder, rape and wife and child abuse are increasing at an alarming rate. It's clear that certain television programs and movies are fostering brutality and murder. As long as they are tolerated, families as well as society suffers.

Sexuality is being despiritualized, coarsened and brutalized. Teen promiscuity, teen pregnancy and venereal diseases are being fostered by television and movies because law makers are afraid of accusations of censorship.

At least parents should keep their children from viewing such harmful stuff by reasoning and appeal. Parents should watch television and movies with their children so that they know what is available and what their children are viewing. Parents should stop their children from watching inappropriate sex and violence. *No excuse by parents is really valid.*

Sibling Rivalry

I used to think that the quarreling between siblings, incessant in some families, was a fact of life that couldn't be avoided. I don't believe that anymore and I don't believe it should be ignored. Various factors influence the kind and degree of conflict between children of the same parents, or between children of divorced parents who have remarried: inborn temperament, relative place in the family, ages, and difference in ages. (In general, the closer the children in age, the greater the tendency for such rivalry.) But most influential is the atmosphere created by the managerial parent.

I remember a family with three young boys close in age who were constantly yelling at each other, hitting each other, calling on the mother for help. She alternated between loud, irritable scolding and grinning helplessly if an adult was present. The grandparents treated the parents to a two-week Florida vacation. The woman hired as a sitter appeared colorless but had a good reputation. She turned out to have a friendly, soft voice and to be a good project inventor and storyteller. Peace immediately settled on the three boys. On a house call I saw them snuggled up against her while she read aloud. The parents could hardly believe her long distance reports but when they returned they were so pleased that they hired the sitter for an extra two weeks. After she left, the quarreling gradually resumed full strength.

The episode startled and educated me. I had had no idea how much the attitude of the caregiver could influence sibling rivalry. And it made me think that it must be at least mildly disturbing to children's personalities to allow wrangling to persist continually.

I don't know all the factors in this case, but I can speculate about a few. The mother probably grew up in a quarreling family and learned that a mother could be helpless to control it. She was, before she started, defeated to a degree; she had lost some of the natural authority of a parent before she had one child; by the time she had three, she was unable to assert any authority at all. Furthermore, she allowed herself to get entangled in her children's quarrels, trying, when appealed to, to find out who was to blame for starting the fight. In my experience, that's always a hopeless quest, because quarreling children can always remember an earlier episode that, they feel, excuses them from their next step. Instead, I think a parent should get close to the angry children, explain in a gentle, sincere manner how sad the quarreling makes her feel. If children soon resume the battle, the parent can ask them to separate for a while, or to sleep and play in different rooms. In other words she shouldn't join in the angry fighting.

Another aspect of quarreling is that unconsciously each child hopes to get the parent to say, "You are my good child. Your brother is a bad child." Though it may seem like putting the cart before the horse, I think that a child often starts fights with the unconscious hope that this time he can get the parent on his side. In other words, the rivalry and the hope of gaining the parents' approval come first, and the fight is a means to this end.

In any case I feel that the parent should avoid taking sides, should avoid anger, and just ask for consideration—that's what the children should feel.

When families belong to a church or synagogue I think children should sometimes attend services and that the clergyman should bring the message of the sermon down to a family level, in a loving, not threatening spirit. When the parents and the children get home the discussion can be continued. I don't mean heavy, disapproving talk but friendly, approving talk. It's good for children to see that spiritual issues can and should be connected to real life situations.

Perhaps you think this is all so obvious that it doesn't need mentioning. Then why are the indices of spiritual well-being plummeting? Why the skyrocketing of marital instability, teenage suicide, violence within the family, teenage pregnancy, drug misuse?

Discipline Through Love

I urge parents to count on mutual love and reasoning as the best ways to motivate a child to behave. These will, in the long run, preserve and enhance the child's spirituality, make him or her the kind of adult who will deal with his or her family, co-workers and others in a friendly, cooperative, honorable way. This, in turn, will bring out the best in other people. I say this not because of a theory, but because I've known dozens of children who were never punished or humiliated and they turned out to be as cooperative and considerate as you could wish.

Shaming, humiliating and shouting angrily at children erodes their self-esteem and is permanently harmful.

Discipline, which to me means the whole parental management of children, and which includes the issue of punishment, is central to the raising of children, in their achieving spirituality and in their being able to pass it on in turn to *their* children.

Physical punishment means hurting children to try to make them behave when other forms of management have failed. It relies ultimately on the parent's superior size and strength. So it teaches that might makes right and that it is acceptable to inflict pain to get one's way. This tends to destroy love and spirituality.

Throughout childhood, but particularly before six years of age, children will be watching their parents and trying to pattern themselves after them. That means not that parents have to be perfect, but that they should show respect for each other and their children, let their spiritual values show, not only in expressing their opinions at the dinner table, but in their attitudes and behavior toward family and friends, toward other groups in the town, the nation and the world.

Parent's tolerance, generosity, affection and their working for a better world are important for the children to see. But most important of all is the parent's expression of love for the children, not only in words but in frequent spontaneous hugs.

Chapter Twelve

Better Schools

For more than 50 years, as a teacher, a parent and an adviser of parents, I've been fascinated with the educational process.

In my opinion, the purpose of education is not to pass tests or to get degrees, but to prepare for life through learning by doing and feeling. In parts of the world where there are no schools, parents encourage children to learn and mature naturally, by giving them opportunities to imitate and assist their parents at their traditional occupations, which children are proud to do.

Where there are schools, the educational process has been formalized into a different kind of process, concentrated on learning for its own sake. Teachers in our traditional schools have accumulated wisdom—as proved by their academic degrees—and they believe their job is to dole it out again, bit by bit, in lectures to students. The students' duty is to memorize it and hand it back at recitation or examination time, and they are graded on how well they do it. Learning is done mainly by words rather than by doing.

In the traditional Arabian village the process is simpler, but the idea is the same: the pupil is taught to recite the Koran from memory. When he—and it's always *he*—accomplishes this feat, he is automatically accepted as a wise man. In our society schools and universities institutionalize this philosophy. Each student collects a package of passing grades each year; at the end of several years she or he turns in the stack of credits for a diploma or degree. Too many students accept this process, not in terms of acquiring wisdom or capability, but as a passport to a better paying job. And too many parents, teachers and employers buy in to the concept as well.

Learning By Doing

In most subjects the best way for students to learn usable knowledge is by some kind of real life activity. Educational reformers, from time to time, have done just that. John Dewey, one of this country's foremost philosophers and educators, called it "learning by doing"; I would add "learning by feeling." Before Dewey, Italian physician and educator Maria Montessori emphasized a form of learning by doing at the child's own pace. Many Montessori schools have expanded Dr. Montessori's techniques by including greater creativity in their curriculum.

As a teacher in medical schools I've seen this principle of learning by doing in action. Long ago medical schools realized that you can't make a physician with lectures or textbooks—although they have some value in the overall process. Medical students have to learn about the human body by dissecting a cadaver. They repeat certain classical experiments in the laboratory. But the crucial step in actually becoming a physician is by diagnosing and treating patients under close supervision.

Dewey advocated in elementary education the project method. Instead of teaching basic subjects separately, teachers apply them to some core project that lets the students explore. The third grader fascinated by Native Americans (calling them Indians just perpetuates a misundertanding that dates back to Columbus) can read books about them and write about them, and learn arithmetic with problems based on what and how they counted. The child can be creative by painting or modeling some aspect of their culture, perhaps in cooperation with other pupils. In the child's social studies, he or she can learn about their customs, travel, and how they kept themselves alive.

If done with imagination and foresight, the project method meets the varying abilities of individual students without making slow learners feel held back, bright students overburdened, or otherwise handicapped pupils left out.

Though I play down the importance of memorization, it does have its place. Children enjoy memorizing when they find pleasure or practical value in doing so, which is why children can recite favorite rhymes or sports records on demand. But nobody ever became an executive or a banker by memorizing spelling rules or multiplication tables, any more than they became a great pitcher by memorizing baseball statistics.

The multiplication tables have to be used in many fields, and spelling is used constantly in most occupations, yet the capability to master them depends largely on inborn capacity for visual memory, which some individuals have to a fantastic degree, while others get along with almost none. George Washington was poor at spelling but he did quite well nevertheless.

Unfortunately, while the project method works well with younger children, it may be harder to fit into higher level classes, especially with today's worldly-wise teenagers. At this stage, learning by doing has to have values that are recognizable by the students, and conventional teaching methods are simply not enough. Effective education demands positive, inspiring teachers with large amounts of imagination and patience.

Getting Past Grades

To make the project method—or any other method, for that matter—work to full advantage, teachers must be well trained and flexible. They must like young people. Classes must be small. Besides books and other teaching aids, schools today need adequate equipment, including computer hardware and software, to engage and stimulate students. Salaries and support budgets must be high enough to draw the best people into teaching and hold them there. Good education takes money, but it pays dividends.

Many teachers, parents and students still operate on the assumption that whatever the course, the higher the grade received, the more the student learned and the more surely she or he is on the road to success in life. Despite the fact that grade point averages and S.A.T. testing are seriously questioned as measures of ability, they are still widely used for college and university acceptance.

Phi Beta Kappa students may, on the average, end up with slightly more prestigious jobs and higher incomes, but there are many exceptions. As a group, the Phi Beta Kappans probably are a little more organized and efficient, but there is no proof that anything they got with their high grades gave them any head start in careers.

The relationship between medical school grades and competence as physicians in practice a number of years later, threw light on this question. A number of general practitioners were objectively reviewed some years after graduation. The study covered the care they took compiling patients' medical histories, the physical examinations they performed, the appropriateness of laboratory tests they ordered, how well they kept up with the medical literature, whether they treated their patients sensitively and kindly, and their overall ability to diagnose and treat patients.

After they were ranked as practicing either superior, average or inferior medicine, they were sorted in terms of their grade ranking in medical school years before. There was no correlation whatsoever. Those practicing superior medicine had come equally from the top, middle, and bottom thirds of their medical school classes, just as did those practicing inferior medicine. What produces capable practitioners is something we vaguely call motivation. Whatever goes into producing it has nothing to do with grades.

I think it's fair to say that grades mislead students and teachers alike. Good grades depend on good memory and a willingness to accept and feed back the teacher's opinions, at least temporarily. Neither of these seems to me important in making a good worker or a good citizen.

But if we abolish grades, how will students know how they are doing? I taught medical students at Western Reserve (it was not yet Case Western Reserve) when grades were abolished. Listening to a few students whimpering over the problem, I realized how we have corrupted students by grading them from school through undergraduate college. They have been made so thoroughly dependent, so passive in their attitude toward the educational process, that they think only someone else can tell them how they are doing. Anyone with a 90 IQ should be able to know how he or she is doing.

More serious is the implication that the students are in schools and universities to satisfy the faculty. The real reason they should be there is because they want to learn something. To be sure, they need guidance. That's why the faculties should encourage them to take initiative and responsibility with electives, independent studies and research of their own choosing.

Part-time Teachers

This country faces a critical shortage of qualified math, science and computer teachers in public schools. The reason is quite simple: we do not pay teachers comparable salaries to their counterparts in the private sector, and there is little likelihood that we will soon do so.

Ironically, where we need teachers most are engineering, computer sciences and other high-tech, well-paid fields. Many such professionals would love to teach one or two courses a week, but our public schools won't allow it. Many of these professionals would volunteer to teach without pay or for a modest fee, and many of their employers would be willing to release them for a few hours a week as a public service, and for good will.

Colleges, especially graduate schools, have for years used part-time or adjunct professors to teach one course at a time. Law schools often hire attorneys to teach a single course. Medical schools use specialists to teach courses in their field of expertise. These gifted professionals often cost less per course than full-time faculty members, providing state-of-the-art expertise and saving money in the process.

Why shouldn't our elementary, middle and high schools do the same thing? Unfortunately, teachers' unions and professional organizations bind state-funded schools in a web of vested interests, prohibiting qualified practitioners from the classroom, while the tenure system protects many less qualified and poorly motivated teachers.

I believe that exposing interested students to serious-minded people who work in trades and professions would help to overcome students' boredom and lethargy. Any such program would have to be organized and supervised by professional educators, and I don't believe that qualified teachers would lose jobs if this proposal were implemented.

Qualification at Every Level

Just as communities insist on certain standards among tradesmen and artisans, a society can't allow professionals to practice without proving competence, particularly in highly technical specialties. When I studied there, Yale Medical School decided to leave examination of students to the National Board of Medical Examiners. The faculty's only function was to be helpful. Besides blunting the paranoid belief that a teacher's main joy is flunking students, the system motivated both faculty and students toward the common goal of achievement.

The same principle of independent final examinations could be applied to students preparing for any occupation. It could provide the public protection from incompetence in everything from medicine and engineering to plumbing and auto repair.

Many trades and professions provide courses, testing and certification within their fields, as do state and local governments. Such testing varies in seriousness and rigor, however, and few independent, nationwide standards apply. National standards, examined objectively in vocational as well as academic subjects, would demand that teachers focus on achievement, not grades, and would motivate students to acquire useful skills and knowledge.

Relieving the Pressure

When I was speaking recently in Japan, educators told me that the rate of suicide in elementary school children was shockingly high and increasing. The reason these children destroy themselves is because they fear that their grades will not satisfy their parents. Later in their school careers, students face the same pressure competing for precious university acceptance, too often with the same tragic results.

We can see how misdirected that kind of pressure is in another society but don't see the comparable mistakes in our own. Fortunately, American children don't take their parents' concern for grades that seriously yet, but I believe that the pressure on the part of schools as well as parents is increasing.

A few years ago President Reagan appointed a "National Commission on Excellence in Education" made up of teachers and administrators at the high school and university levels. Its report showed me how poorly many educators themselves understand the possibilities of education and why so many of our high schools are failing to interest or retain many of their students.

The commission, which deplored the poor state of secondary education, offered three broad recommendations: one more hour of school a day, one more month of school a year, and more homework. In other words, more of the same. But "the same" isn't working—and not because there isn't enough of it.

Experiments long ago showed that homework that repeats work already done in class does not improve students' comprehension or skill—only their grades.

That sort of tedious, unimaginative work is light years behind independent study and independent experiments, performed and evaluated by students, in projects they themselves select and carry out, with minimal supervision but with imaginative guidance by teachers working in supportive rather than dominant roles.

Piling on more of the same will only disillusion these young people earlier and in larger numbers. What they need is a curriculum that starts where their interests are and that rewards them in every class, every day, with some sense of achievement.

There is nothing sacred, however, about the traditional school year. The three-month summer vacation—stretching to four months or more in colleges these days—was predicated decades ago to let rural children work in the fields. Its usefulness is long past, as is the traditional academic semester.

Families with two working parents have difficulty coping with long summer vacations, yet climate-controlled schools make classrooms bearable year round. Public schools willing to offer flexible, challenging curricula could do well to emulate the quarter system used in some colleges: concentrated ten week units of study with a new term starting every three months. The four-term system provides ample holiday breaks, yet allows students to work straight through and graduate earlier if they choose, with the option of taking one term off a year for vacations, jobs or other purposes.

Making Schools Meaningful

One of the most serious problems in high schools—if not the most serious—is the large number of dropouts. In 1990, more than 30 percent of potential graduates dropped out of high school. As the need for unskilled labor declines in the United States, this high dropout rate is doubly tragic.

For the most part, dropouts are not children of educated parents who have stressed the importance of education from the time their children were young. Nor are they children of upwardly mobile parents who themselves did not go to college but are convinced of its great importance.

Dropouts tend to be children of low-income households or single parents, many of whom did not finish high school themselves. These children have not had positive role models to demonstrate the advantages of education or to provide encouragement or motivation. If they come from minority groups or are otherwise discriminated against, they may not even feel they belong to the society. Seeing no advantage in staying in school, resenting criticism and bossing, they just drop out.

I remember a series of interviews in the *Boston Globe* with high school students. By their own accounts they were bored stiff with their school work—and they looked and sounded it. The main difference among them was that students from college educated families took it for granted that they had to graduate from high school and go on to college. The others could at least consider the alternative of dropping out.

Statistics show the price society pays for this trend. Juvenile arrest rates and unemployment figures soar in areas and among groups where dropout rates are highest. Without tangible goals, without hope of permanent employment, without the respect of the greater population, these are truly wasted lives.

Nonetheless, I believe there can be a cure. The particular educational needs for unmotivated students are only larger doses of what all students need—especially during the adolescent years when their impatience or scorn of parents and other adults is at its height.

Money and Maturity

Conservatives in and out of education cry out for a return to "the basics"—reading, writing, spelling, composition, mathematics and history—exactly what they remember studying in their own school days. They scornfully oppose "frills" courses on human relations, sexuality, marriage, health—even driver education and other skills needed to cope with the real world of today.

Some simply want to keep taxes low. Others are uncomfortable about their children looking closely at human feelings. They are scared about how society seems to be moving toward sexual license, drug abuse, abortion, and loss of the old-fashioned religions. The only safety they can see is to go back to what they remember of their childhood.

I, too, am worried about some of the ways our society is moving, but I don't think that running backward with my eyes closed will help.

Children now grow and mature physically at earlier ages than ever. A couple of centuries ago girls reached their first menstrual period at 16 years of age; for girls in America it now comes between ten and 12. Puberty in boys also comes earlier. Yet because of our society's growing need for educated workers, all youths need at least a high school diploma to get any kind of work above the lowliest jobs. At the higher academic and technical levels, our society needs more people with college and post-graduate educations, which keeps young people in universities longer than ever.

This presents young people with an uncomfortable conflict. They feel physically ready for an adult life at progressively younger ages but are kept in school, financially dependent on parents, until they are intellectually and technically qualified. It seems wrong from every point of view for higher education to be limited to children of parents who can afford its ever increasing cost.

A fair solution for such financial stress on the young and on their parents would be for the government to offer college and post-graduate education, as well as a living allowance, to all young people who can demonstrate their ability to use it. This could be provided for in the form of loans or in return for a certain amount of public service, either in military or civilian work. The GI Bill worked this way after World War II and provided returning servicemen with the educational tools needed to develop the nation. America boomed after the war and the GI Bill was one reason for it.

The present system of financing primary and secondary level public education poses two interrelated problems: funds are raised mainly by real estate taxes, making school budgets lowest in economically disadvantaged districts where pupils need inspired schooling most. Homeowners on low incomes, particularly retired people on fixed incomes, are the ones most apt to vote against increases in school taxes.

The solution for both problems is to raise school funds from progressive state or national income taxes on individuals and corporations, disbursed on a per capita basis—just as it is for defense, health care, highway construction, and hundreds of other public services.

Making Your Voice Heard

How does a parent go about influencing a school system—about grades, about competitiveness in general, about too much homework, about making the work more interesting and challenging with projects and with enrichment?

First, you can talk with the teacher when you have a conference; if there are no regular teacher-parent conferences, ask for one. You can't tell the teacher how to teach, but you can tactfully tell him or her your own concerns and ideas.

Attend PTA meetings. If they focus only on bake sales and fund-raising, insist on devoting some of the meetings to the school's philosophy and methods, on what the educators are trying to do in general and in your children's classes in particular. If a majority of parents seem to want change, ask the principal and a school board member to come to at least one meeting.

Go to school board meetings. When there are school board elections, get the candidates to speak to your school PTA. Question them carefully and make your suggestions to them. If there is one candidate with whom you agree heartily, offer to work in his or her election campaign. Candidates are usually desperate for a little help.

Getting Values Back in the Schools

I believe that our society is suffering severely from a loss of spiritual values and that educators from kindergarten to graduate school should let their ideals and beliefs show—not to impose their personal convictions, but to encourage students to discuss them and, most important in today's climate of cynicism, to show that people they respect do have spiritual beliefs.

One of the sharpest criticisms of university students during the outspoken 1960s and 1970s was that classes were so large and impersonal that students never got to know their teachers or what they believed.

Today, when campuses are concerned with "political correctness," many teachers and students alike are afraid to express their views in public for fear that they will be accused of attacking one another, either as individuals or as the entire ethnic, religious or social groups they represent.

I think we need to discuss in schools and universities, as well as at home, today's ethical and spiritual crises: the breakdown of so many marriages, mothers as well as fathers having to work outside the home, excessive competitiveness and materialism, violence, the despiritualization of sexuality, the escalation of criminality and the persistence of discrimination against women and minorities.

As adolescents and youths gradually abandon identification with their parents and find identities of their own, they want to hear the beliefs of people who appeal to them, including the beliefs of their teachers. It's not that they will adopt other people's beliefs uncritically, but will consider them, weigh them against the opinions of others, then reject or adopt them in whole or in part.

It's the same need that a new person on the job feels—to sound out peers or seniors in the hallway, to consult informally about problems. It's the same need that we see in beginning parents when they consult experienced ones over the back fence, in the supermarket or the hardware store.

The reluctance of teachers to reveal their own personal values is deep seated. In part, it reflects the centuries-old struggle to free the universities from the restrictive views of the churches. In the 1990s it also reflects a concern about "political correctness" and fear that a careless word will offend some person or group.

Of course I'm not advocating that teachers speak of their beliefs as if they are the only tenable ones but simply as ideas to be discussed, along with the students' own, when that seems appropriate. Otherwise, if the teacher omits this discussion of his own views it makes students think that values have no importance or that they have no valid connection with other aspects of the subject under discussion.

I'd say that values are the most central aspects of any field, the ones that hold the others together in a constellation. I'd say that all our society's ills—excessive competitiveness and materialism, marital failure, discrimination, drug abuse, violence, the joylessness of work and the despiritualization of sex are partly due to our weakened sense of values or our failure to discuss them.

A few basic qualities are truly valuable in developing individuals who can make useful contributions to the world. They include, in my opinion, a readiness to think for oneself, to try to solve problems, to take initiative and responsibility, to be creative and to be cooperative. It is also essential to be conscientious and to like people.

The first five qualities can be developed in school—if the teachers believe in them and give their students opportunities to practice them every day. The last two come mainly from growing up in a secure, loving family.

Chapter Thirteen

Better Workplaces

At all levels of schooling, from high school through graduate programs, it is important for students to understand the connection between education and work. Our schools often fail to relate the academic curriculum to its intended application later in life. One way to correct that is for young people to be exposed to the workplace at an early age.

I have already recommended that children be exposed to the work their parents do outside the home. In this way, children will develop a more realistic perspective about their parents and themselves, and will be better motivated and prepared for adulthood. Business can play an active role in this process, too. Whether it's a small business donating computers to a local school system, or a major corporation opening new job opportunities for apprentices or interns, the benefits are considerable for everyone.

Apprenticeships

One way to foster learning by doing is to introduce young people to the workplace under the guidance of people already working in occupations. Work-study programs and apprenticeships offer useful alternatives to young people at risk of becoming school dropouts.

Although apprentice programs survive in some city school systems, for the most part they no longer exist. By focusing on knowledge for its own sake and divorcing schools from practical training, we have lost what was once an important bridge from schools to the workplace.

Schools are probably well rid of the old "manual trades" approach that segregated academic students from vocational students at an early age. Although those programs turned out generations of well trained typesetters, bakers and auto mechanics, today's needs are different. Our post-industrial economy needs to foster new skills at all levels. Whether a student aspires to a career in medicine or business management, many of the essential skills are the same, with computer competency at the top of the list.

To be realistic, such programs will always be geared to the non-academically inclined, but they should be totally free of racial or class bias. Just as academic opportunity should be open to all on the basis of ability, so should programs aimed at strengthening the general workforce. In fact, such programs can be particularly beneficial to youths from privileged background who simply are not motivated toward professional careers. It is important that the young people involved—whatever their backgrounds—see the long-term social value as well as the short-term financial rewards of better preparation for work.

Creators of apprenticeship and work-study programs have to recognize and plan for the practical needs of businesses as well as the educational aims of schools. Businesses must have ample opportunity to train potential entry-level employees in essential skills, not just make-work activities. At the same time, students must see tangible rewards for their effort, not meaningless grades. The end result should be a far greater assurance that by the time an adolescent has spent several years being weaned away from the classroom, he or she is ready to become a productive member of the workforce.

Programs that Work

One of the most advanced apprenticeship programs in the world is in Germany, where students combine class work with jobs under the supervision of both educators and employers. Siemens, a German electronics company similar in size and diversity to General Electric, has been training apprentices for more than 100 years. Siemens has a large and growing network of factories in the United States where for three years it has implemented apprenticeship programs.

A few American companies are following the example. Banta, a printing company in central Wisconsin faced an aging workforce and tried several methods of attracting young employees without success, so the company implemented its own apprenticeship program. Banta's apprentices attend high school two days a week and work for three. During a two year program, students pass through all sectors of the printing business, from price estimation and scheduling to presswork, binding and distribution. Each of these areas lets students see how academic skills relate to real work;

for example, estimating a competitive printing job requires math skills to analyze the costs for time and other materials. The apprentices squeeze in a lot of learning but see actual results. They learn by doing.

Blue Cross/Blue Shield of Maine uses job masters to help 15 students a year learn academic and work-related skills. The three-year program starts with the last two years of high school and includes one year of post-high school work, by which time the student is a well-qualified, productive worker. Other health providers offer apprenticeships in hospitals that allow young people to continue their education while they work.

In Boston a program called Protech trains at-risk students for hospital careers, requiring a second year of high school biology and math. One teacher with the program said: "They learn quickly; they have to write well to communicate extremely important information about patient health. The science becomes fascinating when they see how it actually is used by doctors and nurses." Protech is being extended to banking and insurance, with a goal of 2,000 apprentice students by the year 2000.

The benefits are obvious: first and foremost these programs truly educate students to perform in the real world. The problems are real problems, not homework or test questions.

Second, apprenticeship programs discourage dropouts by having them see the relevance of their work. If students can see why they have to use math to plan a printing job, they have a vested interest in getting the numbers right.

Third, employers get a more educated, skilled and dedicated workforce.

Fourth, schools can have smaller classes because apprentices become part-time students, freeing up teacher time for other students. For example, if half of all seniors are in an apprenticeship program and attend school only two days a week, the average class size is reduced by 30 percent.

Day Care at the Workplace

Private day-care centers are common all over America, and some municipalities are starting to offer day care as an adjunct to public schools. In the past few years a number of employers—from large corporations to small businesses—have made on-site day care a reality, and the trend is growing. These employers decided that it was in their own best interests to help their employees, not frustrate them.

For example, Toyota of America in Georgetown, Kentucky, is just one of the companies that has found that workers are happier and more productive when their children are cared for on the premises. Workers can check on their children during breaks, have lunch with them, and give the loving contact children need.

Goldman, Sachs, a Wall Street investment-banking firm, has gone one step further, establishing an on-site emergency center for parents who have a child-care crisis. The motive is to minimize employee absenteeism that happens when the baby sitter is sick or the regular day-care center is closed. The federal government and many Washington, D.C. firms have established day-care facilities at the workplace.

Generally, employers subsidize day care as they do other employee benefits. Parents are encouraged to visit their children during the day, nursing mothers can maintain the normal feeding schedule, and parents can see their older children at play. Children learn to associate with other children and adults, gaining confidence for the transition to school in a few years. Children who commute back and forth to work with mom or dad learn what their parents do for a living. Most importantly, they enjoy the assurance that a parent is always nearby.

The enormous changes in science, technology and communication in my lifetime have revolutionized our work patterns. I believe we need a new, positively-motivated, family-oriented revolution for the twenty-first century. Day care at the workplace is no longer just another perk or a kindness to the employees. A lot of time and resources are lost by employees scrambling to make sure their young children are being cared for properly. If a child-care worker fails to show up, or a day-care facility is closed for a day or more, the worker stays home.

We should encourage the expansion of child-care centers at workplaces—and not just for emergencies. Day care at work should be subsidized with more tax breaks; workers and their unions should demand it. Employers will learn that it is in their own interest in terms of productivity, employee loyalty, and reduced absenteeism. Instead of fragmenting family life, it will strengthen it, and make workers more productive in the process.

Employers should also offer a shorter work week to parents of young children. Studies show that workers can produce as much or more in a focused six-hour workday as in a typical eight-hour day.

Alternative work schedules, such as three- and four-day work weeks, let parents spend more time with their children. Employers will be amazed at how productive workers can be on the job when a shorter work week means less commuting time and more time with spouses and children.

Chapter Fourteen

Better Citizens

If we are to reshape government to serve the people's needs and to fit our country more cooperatively into the world, we need to use our political power at all levels—in our communities, in local and state governments, and nationally.

We could change the whole flavor of life in America by bringing up our children with a spirit of service and kindliness. When young people become committed to causes and activist movements, their ardor and enthusiasm is enormous. Idealistically-motivated young people are quite capable of performing important services and influencing major issues, and often they are more effective at it than their elders. But to get young people actively involved in serious social and political causes, they need to see their parents and other adults serving as role models.

Unfortunately for today's society, many people feel a sense of frustration about influencing their elected leaders and a sense of cynicism about what a single voice or a single vote can accomplish. The American people are quick to voice their opinions on all sides of political and social issues, but too few show a willingness to follow through with real public service, either as voluntary activists or as elected office holders. The country needs both.

Our record at the ballot box is even more appalling. The presidential elections of 1988 and 1992 were sad examples: only half the eligible citizens bothered to go to the polls. Many people figure that when thousands or even millions of votes are being cast, one more doesn't matter. Others are so fed up with the slow, ineffective political process that they consciously withhold their vote as a form of protest. Others simply believe that salvation comes not through politics but through rugged individualism or luck.

Some non-voters are deterred by cumbersome laws on voter registration. Opinion polls show that many don't vote because they doubt the candidates will carry out their promises. This is partly the fault of the candidates, but partly the fault of the citizens for failing to keep pressure on the officials after they are elected. It is easy for candidates to make unrealistic promises they have little intention of carrying out, if they can count on apathy from most of their constituents. But not voting is an indulgence that the wealthy and the powerful don't allow themselves; they know that elections do affect their interests and they generally contribute generously as well as vote.

Once it was possible to buy votes with a few dollars or free drinks at the nearest saloon. Today the political hucksters are much more sophisticated. They know that few people really study the issues and understand the policies that parties and candidates stand for. They know that glib slogans or misleading accusations can sway votes better than serious debate about complex issues.

One reason why the candidates can avoid dealing with the serious issues such as taxation, pollution, defense and foreign relations, is the increasing dependence on hired political consultants who conduct highly persuasive, yet often deceitful, radio and television campaigning. Playing to a desensitized, gullible public, these spin doctors manipulate opinion and turn many people's minds away from real problems to phony, meaningless issues.

Television, unfortunately, lends itself to short glib half-truths, rather than to thoughtful analysis of complex problems. The American public, which now gets most of its information from television screens, has been anesthetized with slick commercials and biased reporting so that many of them can't tell the difference between truth and hokum. They write to television doctors asking for medical advice, or make urgent suggestions to actors on how to untangle the domestic crises of their soap operas. It's no wonder that ordinary entertainers are looked upon as authorities on any subject, and why some of them parlay acting careers into high political office.

Television has taken the political process one step farther away from citizen involvement. When candidates had to stand in front of the electorate and defend their positions in an open give-and-take, they were at least under the obligation to respond to direct questions or dodge the occasional overripe tomato. Today door-to-door stumping and two-way forums are fast disappearing, replaced by quick—and often dirty—recorded sound bites that can be pumped ad nauseum into every household, but with no provision for concerned citizens to respond or ask questions.

One way to prevent sleazy, evasive campaigning would be by a series of genuine debates between the candidates themselves, for two hours each, instead of the shallow, easily evaded questioning by the press that passes for debate now. Another way is to insist that candidates appear before the public—not just before their opponents—ready to field any and all questions on the spot.

My political concerns over the years have not been for quick fixes or special interests, but for causes that will improve the long-term security and well being of all people, particularly children. Besides my opposition to the war in Vietnam, I worked hard for negotiated nuclear disarmament and peaceful relations with the former Soviet Union, and in opposition to nuclear power. The collapse of the Soviet system may have ended the Cold War between the great superpowers, but 40 years worth of nuclear technology and production has only made it easier for paranoid nations—perhaps even drug cartels and international crime syndicates—to get their hands on nuclear weapons.

I am now working for issues that I believe are in the best interests for improving the American society—issues that are the basis for this book:

- ☐ High-quality health care for all;
- ☐ Subsidized day care for children of working parents;
- ☐ Subsidies for parents who stay at home to care for their preschool children;
- ☐ High-quality, challenging schools for all children;
- ☐ Decent housing for every family; and
- ☐ A truly progressive income tax, as it was in the beginning, before all the loopholes were bored into it by special interests.

I've been criticized for getting into politics when people thought I should stick with child care. But I never felt I was getting out of child care. I always felt that my political concerns were quite consistent with my personal beliefs and my professional obligations about children. I'm only ashamed that I was already in my sixties before I realized that politics is an essential arm of pediatrics.

What other way is there to address the outstanding, unmet needs of children in American today? Subsidized high quality day care? It can only be achieved by political activity. Better, more challenging schools, especially in deprived neighborhoods? The answer is politics. Free, high quality health care for all? Politics. How to get rid of the constant risk of nuclear annihilation, the greatest health risk that's ever been faced? Politics. How to relieve malnutrition, decayed housing, neglect and abuse of children? Primarily, the answer is in political action.

Over the years I have supported candidates and policies from our country's two major parties, and I am impatient with both of them. I expect Republican officials to be most attentive to the desires of industrialists and the wealthy, and they generally are. At one time there was a liberal wing of the Republican party that was fairly progressive, but it was overwhelmed by the conservative faction.

The Democratic Party is supposed to be more concerned for the welfare of ordinary citizens, supporting the social security system, Medicare and Medicaid. But in recent years too many Democrats have been trying to prove they are as conservative as Republicans, forgetting their party's dedication to the principle of full employment, civil rights, and the progressive income tax. At a national level, at least, American politics has tended toward the center, where little of deep significance gets done and that only slowly.

Both parties resist using tax revenues for major domestic programs like universal health coverage and expanded child care, but they both have supported huge expenditures for foreign policies, like the Vietnam War and the Gulf War, to support vested corporate interests. Politicians and their party organizations are too concerned with self-preservation and self-perpetuation to address serious issues objectively. Instead, politicians make decisions on the basis of getting re-elected rather than on what's good for the public.

Since 1952, a majority of the American electorate has voted predominantly for Democratic senators, congress people and governors, some of whom were ready to discuss real issues and to argue for progressive policies. Yet the same voters have most often elected conservative Republican presidents, who gave the impression of being above the battle, smiling and reassuring the people in a fatherly way instead of facing issues that really mattered to the masses.

Apparently many Americans now want in their president not a political fighter who expresses alarm and partisanship but a figurehead more like the English monarch, detached from the fray. The best examples are Franklin Roosevelt—though he fought for important social issues at times—Dwight Eisenhower and Ronald Reagan. The only two Democratic presidents in the last quarter century, Jimmy Carter and Bill Clinton, have had real difficulty getting the general populace and the Congress to focus seriously on major social issues.

Another example of distorted politics is the public's wish to revere the presidency, instead of considering it a tough, day-to-day administrative job as originally intended. The exalted image extends to the president's family, especially to the so-called First Ladies, many of whom have been pragmatic, behind-the-scenes influencers of policy. A majority of American women, polled on what woman they admire most, name the president's wife, no matter what kind of person she is or what she stands for. Perhaps opinion will shift by the time we have our first First Gentleman.

I blame the press for the lack of attention to the issues. They pay the most attention during a presidential campaign to the relative positions of the two candidates and on who's gaining or losing, as if it was a horse race or the World Series. This only fuels the passion of many voters to back a winner, not to vote on issues that might actually improve their lives and the lives of their children and grandchildren.

The low point of Professor Barry Commoner's campaign for the presidency on the Citizens Party ticket in 1980, in which I was the vice presidential candidate, was, he said, when a puzzled interviewer asked, "Professor Commoner, are you a serious candidate or are you only interested in the issues?"

Serious alternative candidates, unless they are backed with huge personal fortunes like the abortive effort of Ross Perot, are lost in the undertow. I can speak from personal experience, having weathered a national political campaign trying to get my voice heard.

Citizen Activism

The economic health of the nation depends on broad political issues such as peace and war, disarmament, free trade, unionization, and taxation. Good day care, health care and schools can only be gained by political activity, starting at the community level, by parents and other concerned citizens. People need to learn these truths, from grade school onward, so that voting will seem an important privilege.

Election laws need to be changed in a number of ways. The most important is for universal voter registration so that the entire electorate can participate. Campaign contributions and political action committees must be regulated, to deprive big industries and corporations of their enormous, disproportionate power to buy political influence. That reform will take vigorous political activity on the part of ordinary citizens.

Television and radio stations should be required to donate appreciable chunks of time at elections for candidates to debate each other in depth—not 15-second spots that favor glib distortion of the issues. Broadcasting stations should also provide time for citizens to confront politicians directly about the issues that affect them. We must remember that television and radio stations are given free use of the public airways and permitted to sell commercial time. For this economic benefit they can and should be forced to provide time to promote democracy in action.

This is as important for local government and school board elections as it is for state and national campaigns. Local political debate and grassroots activism are vital to a truly democratic process, because persistent local issues soon echo on the larger political stage. Local politicians who find themselves pressed for community day care, for example, will soon turn to county and state political organizations for guidance and support.

It is just as important for parents to stay politically active between elections as it is for them to vote. You can make your opinion known with a letter to the editor of your local paper or a call to a call-in talk show. You can write letters to mayors and city councils, to state representatives and governors, to your senator and congress person, even to the president—not once but every time you get hot under the collar. You can attend public meetings and raise issues from the floor.

It's surprising how few people—even among those deeply committed to an issue—have ever written to elected officials, though office holders all admit that mail has an impact. A personal letter in your own words is far more effective than another signature on a form letter from a pressure group. Don't worry about eloquence or punctuation; just make clear which side of the issues you are on. You can locate the addresses of city and county offices with a phone book, and you can lobby your senators and representative in Washington through his or her local office.

Organize a committee and give it a name. Formal group resolutions and petitions with pages of signatures begin to get officials' attention. If polite pressure falls on deaf ears and you feel strongly that your elected official is still off base, you can picket his or her office with signs and loudspeakers. Open meetings and picketing are likely to draw newspaper or television coverage, which can give you more of a chance to make your views public. Picketing takes a little courage the first time you do it. Try to include at least one clergyman to lend dignity and morality to your cause. If the issue concerns children, they can come along too.

If you feel that government has been criminally wrong in vital matters—whether it's neglect of the homeless locally or a national issue like a military incursion—and you have voted, lobbied, written letters to officials and to the editor, I feel that you are justified in committing non-violent civil disobedience in a demonstration. It usually results in a night in jail and a $25 fine; but there is no doubt that it gets many times more media attention than a polite demonstration.

Political Choices

All sociological studies agree that the greater a person's wealth or income, the more likely he or she is to be politically conservative, voting for the candidates who promise to keep expenditures and taxes down, irrespective of their positions on other issues. They want, above all, to keep the material advantages they have or hope for. Some of them see progressive politicians as revolutionaries, labor leaders as robbers, and the poor as lazy, boozing bums.

A great majority of physicians and lawyers in private practice are politically conservative, both because they earn high incomes and because they are dependent on their individual efforts. The same is true of successful business people and corporate executives. Among their counterparts employed full time by medical, law and business schools, on the other hand, there are a fair percentage of progressives.

The conservative position is also shared by people who earn only modest incomes. Their conservatism is based on a strong sense of personal independence, a distrust of collective efforts in general, and a distaste for having to pay taxes to help the less fortunate. They take pride in their hard work and individual efforts in spite of the uncertainties of their economic position.

Many of the skilled, unionized workers were the largest group in the Democratic Party in the depressed

1930s and 1940s because they felt neglected. Now, many of them vote Republican, because they were relatively prosperous from the 1950s to the 1980s, but now feel threatened by the attention given to African-Americans and Hispanics.

How can we hope to overcome the tendency of these people to vote for the candidate who projects a pleasing personality, who oversimplifies complex issues, who distances himself from squabbles over policies? What defense is there against the candidate who deliberately stirs up paranoid attitudes by picturing his opponent as unpatriotic, a dupe of the communists, an enemy of religion and decency? Surely it will be a difficult long-term effort.

Involving Children

The way to lessen the susceptibility to paranoid campaigning—as well as to raise citizens who are generally good workers, good parents and good neighbors—is to bring up children so that they feel loved, secure, and unthreatened by hostile forces.

Since poverty and discrimination sow the seeds for many other social ills—neglect of children, crime, alienation from the society instead of identification with it—ordinary citizens working through their government must eliminate poverty. This can be accomplished by providing work for everyone, either in private industry, constructive government projects, or by allowances such as the negative income tax, a far better solution than conventional welfare payments, which offer little return to the country as a whole.

Along with career-oriented courses, schools and universities should teach the realities of politics today, not just the idealized, laundered concepts tailored for politically-correct text books. Young people should know how our political parties evolved and what they stand for today, if anything. They should understand the political power exerted by corporate America and political action groups through their large contributions to campaign funds. They need to appreciate the power of television campaigning, to see examples of how the political sound bites distort the opponent's position, the shallowness of so-called debates, the press's preoccupation with the standing of the candidates in the opinion polls, and the voters' preoccupation with candidates' personalities rather than with the issues.

Civics and political science classes that put on mock election campaigns let young people begin to see the dynamics of real differences of opinion. Debating their classmates, researching and taking positions on issues, they begin to understand the difference between give-and-take and standing fast. Studying the analysis of the election results, they see what people say about how they voted. Such exercises make students realize the rationality and the illogic of voting behavior as they get ready to vote themselves.

Establishing in young children a strong sense of values and a high standard of personal behavior builds their self-confidence. With inner security and self-confidence, young people can explore and absorb a wide range of ideas without prejudice. As adults they will be able to think for themselves, make sound decisions in their own lives, and contribute to a better society.

In the end, the way to a better world for our children is through our children themselves.

Chapter Fifteen

Can We Make a Better World for Our Children?

Am I a pessimist or an optimist about the future of our country? It depends. Right now we are on the skids—we are neglecting our children emotionally and educationally, marriage is increasingly unstable, we are slipping deeper and deeper into acceptance of violence, we are losing our sustaining spiritual beliefs and we are absorbed in materialism and competitiveness. If we allow these trends to continue I see us slipping further into chaos.

On the other hand, we have the means to save our society—enough funds to subsidize mothers or fathers who want to stay at home to care for their preschool children, to subsidize better day-care centers and schools.

We have a skilled work force in most fields and a high proportion of college graduates. We have boundless natural resources and creative talent. In other words, we have the means to begin a progressive improvement in all aspects of our society *provided* that parents see the importance of encouraging more kindliness, helpfulness and lovingness—less selfishness—in their young children. This is only partly to sweeten their manners or to improve their souls. It's more to help them develop into adults inclined in their deepest nature to be sensitive and responsive to the needs—spiritual and practical—of those around them.

The other major provision for a better world is that parents become much more politically active. They should vote—and vote discriminately. They should contribute funds to and help in the offices of worthy candidates, local, state and national. They should keep after their officials after they are elected, whether or not they voted for them. They should keep after them with letters and lobbying, whether at a local or a Washington office, with letters to the editor and with demonstrations. A demonstration by five people with five signs in front of an official's office can make a strong impression.

How else than by political activity are we going to get children's most desperate needs met? How are we going to get subsidies for parents who want to stay at home to care for their preschool children? How are we going to get subsidies for more high quality day care? How are we going to get better schools and health care? Most of these can only be accomplished through political activity.

Lastly, I believe that in the long run, the spiritual needs of the family—and of the nation—must be met not only by less absorption in making money and gaining "advancement" but by people coming to realize that child care, the happiness of the family, the feelings of adults and children and cultural and neighborhood activities are the most vital aspects of existence.

Can we make a better world for our children? I believe we can, if enough people are concerned and get involved in changing what is wrong with society. I can't do it by myself—I can only provide my suggestions to help nudge us toward the right goals.

It's up to each of us to help create a better world for our children.

Notes

Chapter Two

1. *New York Times*, March 14, 1994, D-6.
2. *USA Today*, August 27, 1993, House Budget Committee, *Economic Report of the President.*

Chapter Four

1. *Los Angeles Times*, November 5, 1993.
2. American Psychological Association as quoted in *Newsweek* magazine, July 12, 1993, p. 65.

Chapter Five

1. *Jerusalem Post,* "First Graders Run Into Weight Problems," November 24, 1992.
2. *London Times,* "Switch Off That Thing and Get Outside," November 11, 1992.

Chapter Ten

1. San Francisco Planning Code Section 165, P.L. 86.1, August, 1987.

A
Abortion, 98, 174
Absenteeism, 186, 187
Actors, 191
Adolescence, 111, 113-117, 137, 153, 166, 178, 183
Advertising, 59, 81, 115, 121, 151, 191
African-Americans, 73, 200
Agnosticism, 120, 138
Alcohol, 66
American Psychological Association, 207
Andover Academy, 24
Anthropology, 100
Apathy, 190
Apprenticeship programs, 133 181, 182, 183, 184
Architecture, 125
Arkansas, 35, 36
Arts, 120, 121, 125
Athletic scholarships, 56
Austria, 66
Automobile industry, 48

B
Baby and Child Care, 15, 27, 28, 29, 30, 33, 35
Banta Printing, 183
Biology, 100, 107, 124, 184
Blue Cross/Blue Shield, 184
Boredom, 55, 169
Boston Globe, 173
Boston, Massachusetts, 184
Boycotts, 81
Breast feeding, 27, 30
British Virgin Islands, 36
Bryn Mawr College, 25
Business school, 199

C
California, 29
California Institute of Technology, 76
Camden, Maine, 36
Canada, 73
Cancer, 84
Care and Feeding of Children, 20
Carnegie, Andrew, 119
Carter, Jimmy, 195
Cartoons, 77
Censorship, 98, 114, 157
Charity, 148, 153
Cheney, Jane, 24, 25, 35
Child abuse, 157, 193
Child support, 63
Children's Television Resource and Education Center, 76
Childrens Hospital of the East Bay, Oakland, CA 29
Christianity, 99
Christmas, 152, 154
Cigarettes, 67, 68
Citizens Party, 196
Civil rights, 194
Cleveland, Ohio, 30
Clinton, Bill, 195
Cliquishness, 110
Cold War, 47, 192
College, 56, 57, 88, 168-173, 75, 177, 201
College of Physicians and Surgeons, Columbia University, 26
Columbia University, 25, 26
Comic books, 110, 119
Commoner, Barry, 196
Competitiveness, 45, 48, 52-58, 66, 69, 88, 101, 124, 132, 133, 135, 176, 178, 179

Computers, 51, 75, 76, 96, 119, 166, 168, 169
Congress, 134
Connecticut, 20, 24
Constitution, 123
Contraception, 114, 115
Coronary heart disease, 84, 85
Counseling, 64, 136, 145, 147
Crime, 52, 59, 60, 70, 74, 80, 157, 174, 178, 192, 200
Crushes, 110
Cults, 60
Cynicism, 123, 124, 151, 177, 189

D

Dance, 125
Day care, 35, 45, 51, 53, 70, 135, 153, 185, 186, 193, 196, 197
Democrats, 33, 34, 47, 194, 195, 199
Demonstrating, 198
Depression, 27, 84
Detroit, Michigan, 29
Dewey, John, 164
Diabetes, 83
Diet, 83, 84, 86, 87
Discipline, 145, 161
Discrimination, 173, 178, 179, 200
Divorce, 34, 35, 45, 59, 60, 62, 63, 135, 144, 147, 177, 179
Documentaries, 81
Double-income families, 172, 177, 185
Doubleday, 27
Downsizing, 60
Drama, 119, 125
Drop-outs, 52, 173, 174, 181, 184
Drug abuse, 34
Drugs, 56, 60, 66, 67, 85, 86, 160, 174, 179, 192

E

Economic depressions, 59
Economic Report of the President, 207
Education, 48, 124, 134, 153, 163-170, 172-179, 181, 182, 193, 196, 201
Eisenhower, Dwight D., 195
Elderly, 93, 148
Elementary school, 165, 169, 171
Employee benefits, 51
Engineering, 169
Environment, 153
Evolution, 121
Exercise, 84, 88, 89, 148

F

Fads, 66
Family meetings, 147
Fat foods, 84
Feminism, 33, 35
Films, 64, 80, 97, 115
First Ladies, 195
Food stamps, 47
Formality, 94
France, 24
Freudianism, 27, 66, 103, 104, 117
Frisbees, 56
Fundamentalism, 98

G
Georgetown, Kentucky, 186
Germany, 183
GI Bill, 175
Goldman, Sachs, 186
Goldwater, Barry, 31
Grades, 53, 132, 163, 164, 166, 167, 171, 176, 183
Graduate school, 169, 175, 177, 181
Great Depression, 46
Guilt, 21, 22, 23
Gulf War, 194

H
Health, 51
Health care, 35, 46, 47, 48, 134, 176, 193, 194, 196
Helpfulness, 136, 154, 156
High blood pressure, 83
High cholesterol, 84, 85, 86
High school, 57, 88, 131, 153, 168, 169, 171, 173, 181, 184
Hispanics, 200
Homelessness, 47, 148, 198
Homework, 53, 171, 176, 184
House Budget Committee, 207
Housing, 193
Hugs, 136, 161
Humanism, 123
Humphrey, Hubert, 33
Hyperactivity, 86, 87

I
IBM, 60
Idealism, 23, 34, 45, 97, 98, 100, 104, 116, 117, 120, 121, 122, 124, 134, 156, 189
Ideals, 110, 115
Imaginary companions, 110
Income taxation, 193, 194, 196, 200
Industrialization, 49
Instant gratification, 32
Islam, 99
Israel, 58, 83
Italy, 164

J
Japan, 66, 171
Jerusalem Post, 207
Job training, 134
Johnson, Lyndon B., 22, 31
Joint disease, 83
Judaism, 99

K
Kentucky, 186
Kibbutzim, 58
Kindergarten, 177
Kindness, 136, 151, 154, 156, 189
Kinsey Report, 113
Koran, 163

L
Law school, 169, 199
Lead poisoning, 47
Literature, 119, 125
Little Rock, Arkansas, 35
London Times, 207
Los Angeles Times, 207

M
Maine, 23, 36, 184
Malnutrition, 47
Manic depressive psychosis, 26
Marriage, 58, 62, 63, 66, 101,

103, 108, 112, 116, 117, 122, 124, 144, 160, 174, 177, 179
Massachusetts, 184
Massage, 148
Masturbation, 21
Materialism, 45, 46, 50, 57, 58, 69, 98, 100, 120, 124, 135, 151, 178, 179
Mathematics, 168, 184
Mayo Clinic, University of Minnesota, 29
McDonough, Tom, 76
Meals, 147
Medicaid, 194
Medical school, 25, 131, 164, 167, 169, 170, 199
Medicare, 194
Meditation, 87, 136, 148
Memorization, 165, 168
Mental illness, 59
Michigan, 29
Middle Ages, 57
Middle school, 169
Mobility, 50, 69
Montessori, Maria, 164
Montessori schools, 164
Morality, 21
Morgan, Mary, 35, 36, 144
Motivation, 54, 167
Movies, 119, 157
Murder, 74, 80, 157
Music, 95, 121, 125
Mutilation dreams, 109

N

National Board of Medical Examiners, 170
National Commission on Excellence in Education, 171
National Commission for a Sane Nuclear Policy (SANE), 30, 31
National Peoples Party, 33
Native Americans, 73, 165
Navy, 70, 71
Neglect, 52, 53, 70, 135, 193, 200
New Haven, Connecticut, 20, 24
New York, 23, 25, 26, 32
New York Hospital, 26
New York Nursery and Child's Hospital, 26
New York Times, 207
Newsweek magazine, 207
Nixon, Richard M., 33
Nuclear arms race, 35
Nuclear disarmament, 192, 196
Nuclear disarmament movement, 31
Nuclear power, 192
Nuclear testing, 30
Nuclear war, 60, 193
Nuclear weapons, 192

O

Oakland, CA., 29
Obesity, 83, 84, 86
Ohio, 30
Olympic trials, 1924, 24
Outings, 149

P

Pacifiers, 28
Page, Parker, 76
Painting, 95
Parent identification, 105-109,

117
Parent identification/ idealization, 121, 178
Paris, France, 24
Part-time employment, 51
Patriotism, 32, 57
Peale, Norman Vincent, 32
Pediatrics, 26, 27, 29, 33, 34, 136, 156, 193
Peer pressure, 68, 115
Penis envy, 108, 109
Pennsylvania, 24, 29
Pensions, 46
Permissiveness, 33
Perot, H. Ross, 196
Philadelphia, Pennsylvania, 24
Physical punishment, 132
Physics, 107
Picketing, 198
Pittsburgh, Pennsylvania, 29
Play, 54, 81, 88, 89, 106
Playing doctor, 107
Pocket Books, 28
Poetry, 121, 125
Political activism, 31, 32, 33, 34, 35, 150, 153, 189, 192, 193, 197, 199
Political correctness, 177, 178, 201
Political participation, 133
Pop music, 95
Pornography, 65
Poverty, 45, 47, 49, 70, 200
Power, 120
Prayer, 148
Presbyterian Hospital, New York, 26
Preschool, 53
Presidents Council for Fitness, 89
Project method, 165, 166, 172, 176
Protech, 184
Psychiatry, 26, 29, 70, 87, 145
Psychoanalysis, 26, 103, 104, 109, 117
Psychology, 23, 25, 76, 80, 83, 100, 124
Psychopaths, 71
Puberty, 175
Public service, 189
Punishment, 160, 161

Q
Quarreling, 136, 158, 159
Quiet Time, 148

R
Racism, 73, 200
Radio, 191, 197
Rape, 74, 157
Reagan, Ronald, 171, 195
Recreation, 45, 50, 54, 55, 56, 57, 148
Religion, 57, 60, 97-99, 101, 103, 107, 111, 115, 119, 120, 123, 137-139, 147, 155, 160, 174, 178, 198
Republicans, 24, 31, 34, 47, 194, 195, 200
Ritalin, 86, 87
Role models, 119, 120, 121, 154, 156, 161
Roosevelt, Franklin D., 195
Russia, 48, 192

S
San Francisco, CA., 207
S.A.T.s, 166
Schizophrenia, 26
School lunch programs, 47
Schools, 35, 131
Science, 48, 99, 103, 109, 124, 125, 138, 168, 184, 186
Scolding, 147, 156, 158, 161
Sears, 60
Second marriages, 62
Security blankets, 30
Sex education, 65, 98, 114, 115
Sexual abuse, 74
Sexual role-reversal, 130
Sexuality, 21, 64, 65, 98, 100, 103, 104, 106, 110, 112-117, 157, 174, 178, 179
Sibling rivalry, 158, 159
Siemens, 183
Single-parent families, 93
Singles clubs, 62
Slavery, 73
Smoking, 68
Snacking, 84
Social security, 194
Social work, 145
Socialism, 25, 48
Sociopathy, 71
Soviet Union, 30
Space Adventure, 76
Spiritual values, 50, 52, 57, 59, 65, 100, 101, 103, 107, 112, 114-116, 119-124, 135-137, 139, 151, 155-157, 161, 177
Spock, John, 26
Spock, Michael, 26
Sports, 54, 55, 56, 88
Stardom, 55
Stay-at-home parents, 52, 193
Stepparenting, 64, 144, 145
Steroids, 56
Stroke, 84, 85
Stuffed animals, 30
Suicide, 34, 59, 160, 171
Sunday school, 138-140
Supreme Court, 65

T
Technology, 48, 52, 96, 114, 125, 186
Teenage pregnancy, 34, 112, 114, 157, 160
Television, 49, 55, 74-78, 80, 81 84, 87, 96, 97, 110, 115, 119, 135, 148, 150,151, 157, 191,197, 201
Television news, 49, 74, 78, 79
Television violence, 75, 76, 77, 78, 80, 81, 157
Third World, 49
Thomas, Norman, 25
Three Stooges, 82
Thumb sucking, 27
Toilet training, 27, 30
Toy guns, 81
Toyota of America, 186

U
Unconsciousness, 104, 117, 159
Unemployment, 52, 59, 174
United Nations, 32
University of Minnesota, 29
University of Pittsburgh, 29
USA Today, 207

V

Vacations, 149, 172
Vaccinations, 47
Values, 45, 97, 98, 101, 111, 120-123, 134, 147, 157, 177, 179, 201
Vassar College, 22
Victorianism, 100
Video cassette recorder, 141
Video games, 75
Videos, 97, 151
Vietnam War, 22, 31, 32, 34, 192, 194
Violence, 34, 45, 60, 73, 75-78, 80, 81, 101, 135, 157, 160, 178, 179
Volunteerism, 148, 153, 169, 190
Voting, 190, 196, 198, 201
Vulgarity, 96, 97, 110

W

Wall Street, 119, 186
Wardrobe, 94, 95, 100
Washington, George, 166
Wayne University, 29
Weaning, 27, 30
Welfare, 200
Western Reserve University, 30, 31, 168
Wife abuse, 157
Wisconsin, 183
Work-study programs, 181, 182, 183, 184
World War I, 22
World War II, 46, 70, 175

Y

Yale Medical School, 25, 170
Yale University, 20, 24, 32
Yoga, 148